v. S.

eine (obwohl diese nicht Mozart's Handschrift)
...a, Voell. Durch. Köchel No 617.

ALSO BY COREY MEAD

War Play:

Video Games and the

Future of Armed Conflict

THE STORY OF
BENJAMIN FRANKLIN'S
GLASS ARMONICA

ANGELIC MUSIC

COREY MEAD

SIMON & SCHUSTER

NEW YORK   LONDON   TORONTO   SYDNEY   NEW DELHI

Simon & Schuster
1230 Avenue of the Americas
New York, NY 10020

First Simon & Schuster hardcover edition October 2016

SIMON & SCHUSTER and colophon are
registered trademarks of Simon & Schuster, Inc.

For information about special discounts for bulk purchases,
please contact Simon & Schuster Special Sales at 1-866-506-1949
or business@simonandschuster.com.

The Simon & Schuster Speakers Bureau can bring authors to your live event.
For more information or to book an event, contact the
Simon & Schuster Speakers Bureau at 1-866-248-3049
or visit our website at www.simonspeakers.com.

Interior design by Ruth Lee-Mui

Manufactured in the United States of America

1   3   5   7   9   10   8   6   4   2

Library of Congress Control Number: 2016000734

ISBN 978-1-4767-8303-1
ISBN 978-1-4767-8307-9 (ebook)

To Mom, Dad, and Ken

CONTENTS

CONTENTS

6

THE ARMONICA IN GERMANY AND AMERICA 123

7

MESMER AND THE ARMONICA 133

8

THE ARMONICA FADES INTO OBSCURITY 159

9

THE ARMONICA'S REVIVAL 187

AUTHOR'S NOTE

T he book you are about to read may
seem unusual. It is, in the main, the story of a musical instrument, a unique, ethereal-sounding creation that was devised by
America's most inventive Founding Father. And yet this instrument's curious history provides us with a window into any number of worlds beyond music: It tells us about eighteenth- and
nineteenth-century culture, psychology, and mysticism, about
how styles come and go, and about the various prejudices and
beliefs that have always attached themselves to music, and to
every other form of art.

As much as anything, I hope this book is *fun*—that it en-
tertains you, and that it takes you on an unexpected journey
through one of the unknown legacies of Benjamin Franklin,

arguably the most widely skilled individual this country has ever produced. I hope the book tells lots of things you've never heard before. Most of all, I hope it stirs in you some of the same wonder and enchantment that, for me, a great piece of music has always generated.

INTRODUCTION

In the 1740s, as a middle-aged man, Benjamin Franklin was journeying through the Allegheny Mountains when he chanced upon a scene that remained with him for decades afterward. An impoverished Scots family—husband, wife, and teenage daughter—were gathered on their front porch in the fading evening light. As Franklin sat with the family, the wife began singing a haunting, wistful tune, "Sae Merry as We Twa Ha'e Been" ("Such Merry as We Two Have Been"):

> *A lass that was laden'd with care*
> *Sat heavily under yon thorn*
> *I listen'd a while for to hear*
> *When thus she began for to mourn*

When e'er my dear shepherd was there

The birds did melodiously sing

And cold nipping winter did wear

A face that resembled the Spring

Sae merry as we twa ha'e been

My heart it is like for to break

When I think on the days we ha'e seen

The wife's soft, harmonious voice, along with the melancholy lyrics, brought Franklin to tears. Thirty years later, living in Passy as the American ambassador to France, and relating the story to his French friend André Morellet, Franklin remained moved by the memory.

Though he is known as a scientist and statesman, Benjamin Franklin had a lifelong appreciation for the power of music and song. And while he is renowned for such ingenious inventions as bifocals, the Franklin stove, the lightning rod, and the odometer, his own favorite invention, the one that he said gave him the "greatest personal satisfaction," was a musical instrument. It was called the glass armonica, and while the instrument is largely unknown to the general public today, it was so popular in the late eighteenth and early nineteenth centuries that

Mozart, Beethoven, and Handel wrote works for it, Marie Antoinette and numerous European monarchs played it, Goethe
and Thomas Jefferson praised it, and Dr. Franz Mesmer used it
as an integral part of his Mesmerism sessions. Most remarkably
of all, the glass armonica was the first musical instrument ever
invented by an American, making it not only an important ele-
ment of Franklin's legacy, but a crucial part of early American
culture. During the initial decades of its popularity, over 5,000
armonicas were produced in factories throughout Europe, and
more than 500 pieces were composed for it.

The glass armonica became Franklin's lifelong companion;
he played it in his home in Philadelphia, and during his many
years of residency in Europe. The instrument meant so much
to him that he planned on dedicating an entire chapter of his
never completed autobiography to its invention. Even at the end
of his life, Franklin declared the glass armonica to be his most
cherished creation.

The armonica appeared at a time when the world's population was exploding, and with that explosion came a rapid
upsurge in the number of instrument makers, as well as the
inventiveness and resourcefulness these makers needed to com-
pete in a crowded field. The number of musicians, the quantity

of performed music, the money spent on music, and the distri-bution of printed music were swiftly expanding, as well. For a period of time in the late eighteenth century, the glass armonica seemed, in scholar Heather Hadlock's words, to "conjure up all the magic of which music was capable." Like the "magic rattle" envisioned by philosopher Ernst Bloch, the armonica gave the impression of being an instrument both sacred and occult, one that could either summon beneficent spirits or banish evil ones through the power of its materiality. "Like Orpheus's lyre," Had-lock writes, the armonica "was no mere object for making music, but a focus for fantasies about ideal music itself." Drugstores stocked their shelves with special armonica water that contained "secret" ingredients (likely just alcohol) to help musicians play better. A large glass armonica factory in Germany employed dozens of workers to churn out hundreds of instruments.

With the onset of the nineteenth century, the armonica be-came a popular symbol for Romantic writers, who viewed it as an awe-inspiring emblem of all that was mysterious, seductive, and transcendent about the supernatural realm. Take the author, composer, and music critic E. T. A. Hoffmann's fictional Kapell-meister Kreisler, the writer's alter ego, who describes a young singer's voice pouring "heavenly balm into the wounds inflicted on the tortured musical schoolmaster that I am. . . . Her long-held, swelling armonica notes transport me into heaven." In his 1997 novel *Mason & Dixon*, Thomas Pynchon picked up on this theme, writing of the armonica, "If Chimes could whisper, if Melodies could pass away, and their souls wander the Earth . . . if Ghosts danced at Ghost Ridottoes, 'twould require such Musick . . . ever at the edge of breaking forth, in Fragments, as Glass breaks."

Eventually Franklin's instrument fell out of popular favor, partly due to claims that its haunting sounds could drive musicians out of their minds. Some players fell ill, complaining of nervousness, muscle spasms, and cramps. Audiences were also susceptible; following an incident in Germany in which a child died during an armonica performance, the instrument was even banned in several rural towns. Some people thought the instrument's ethereal tones summoned the spirits of the dead, or had magical powers. Franklin himself ignored this controversy, but the armonica never regained its early status as one of the eighteenth century's most celebrated instruments.

After lingering in obscurity for a century and a half, the instrument has in recent decades enjoyed a revival, as a small group of dedicated musicians has labored to bring the glass armonica

Eighteenth-century drawing of a glass armonica.

back into the public consciousness. In the last twenty years composers have written pieces for it in genres ranging from chamber music and opera to electronic and popular music.

In the following pages, I tell the full tale of the instrument's rise and fall—and rise. It is a story that spans Revolutionary America, England, and the capitals of Europe, and it includes many of the most famous and fascinating figures of its day. Entertainment is foremost in a journey like this, but the journey also provides us with a unique and intimate portrait of the period.

1

THE ANGELICK ORGAN:
A HISTORY OF THE
MUSICAL GLASSES

He was an inventor, an eccentric, a relentless self-promoter. Those who admired him described his restless character as quixotic; those who didn't called him an "enterprising scoundrel." He pursued a lifetime of failed schemes, many of them outlandish. An inveterate writer, he published late in life a soon forgotten "Miscellaneous Works" and a volume of poetry. Yet his sole success—an innovative arrangement of musical glasses—would find resonance decades later in the life of one of the world's most famous men.

The inventor's name was Richard Pockrich, and he was born into a large inheritance on his family's sprawling estate in Derrylusk, Ireland, in 1695. Benjamin Franklin knew of him, noting in a letter that the musical glasses had been invented by a "gentleman from Ireland" named "Pockeridge." Pockrich's father, a member of Parliament, had a been a military hero, a noted commander during the Williamite wars for the Irish Crown, and was grievously injured during the siege of Athlone five years before his son's birth.

As a young man, Richard inherited from his father an estate worth between £1,000 and £4,000 per year. Though he never served in the military, young "Captain Pockrich," as he liked to be called, frittered away these substantial funds on a series of ideas and inventions that were often dismissed, even ridiculed, by many of his contemporaries. Not all of his plans, however, were wild. In 1715, Pockrich, barely out of his teens, moved to Dublin, where he opened near Islandbridge a brewery and distillery, which eventually folded. (Undeterred, the Captain never lost his passion for brewing or drink. When, years later, he lost a competition for the Royal Dublin Society's best barrel of ale, Pockrich's friends reported that he "consoled himself by philosophically and courageously drinking his own brew.") He also ran twice for Parliament and lost, and pursued a futile campaign to be Master of the Choristers of Armagh Cathedral.

Pockrich dreamed of returning life to the bogs of Ireland by draining them and establishing vineyards in their stead. He wrote vigorous pamphlets exhorting the wisdom of his idea, and tried without success to interest Parliament in bankrolling his plan. He also disgorged a good part of his fortune on a scheme to raise geese on miles of infertile mountain land, declaring that, if successful, he could supply the whole market for fowl in Great Britain, Ireland, and France.

In one surprisingly sensible proposal, Pockrich outlined a method for rejuvenating wrinkled skin. "Take common brown paper," he wrote, "steep it in vinegar, then apply it to the forehead, the skin about the eyes, or any other wrinkled part; let it lie on some time, every half hour renewing the application. The wrinkles not only disappear, but the cheeks glow with a vermeil that excels the power of paint." As it happens, his method is not only workable, it is similar to treatments used today.

Other proposals indicated the scope of his ambitions. He developed a plan to provide all men and women with wings for flying. If given the necessary money, Pockrich argued, the day would soon come when humans would never think again of walking. He was an early and fervent proponent of blood transfusions, claiming that he could cure infirmities and greatly extend the lifespan by using tubes or pipes to connect the sick and the elderly with the healthy and young. The pumped-in blood of a "strong healthy cook maid, or a kitchen wench" would surely revivify those at death's doorstep. So confident was Pockrich of his abilities that one lawmaker who knew him jokingly urged Parliament to issue a decree stating that "anyone attaining the age of 999 years shall be deemed to all Intents and Purposes dead in law." This would ensure that relatives of these ancient but sprightly humans could still claim their inheritance, and that vicars would still receive "burial fees" from their immortal, but legally dead, parishioners.

Pockrich also had a touch of the visionary in him. At a time when ships were made entirely of wood, he proposed building unsinkable metal-hulled ships for the major powers' navies—an invention that did not appear until nearly a century later. In the realm of the arts, he envisioned an orchestra of many-sized drums, all varied in tone, which would be placed in a circle and played by a lone drummer in the middle.

In 1741, when he was in his late forties, Pockrich finally hit upon the invention, or reinvention, that changed his life, and for which he is now remembered. Improvising upon a long tradition of glass-based musical instruments, Pockrich developed what he called his "angelick organ." In the beginning, he played his organ using wooden sticks, much as a related instrument, the glasspiel or vérillon, had been played in years previous. Eventually Pockrich discarded his sticks and began playing the instrument as one rubs a wineglass, with wet fingers tracing the rim.

Ever the self-promoter, he advertised himself as a "virtuoso" of this celestial-sounding instrument. Financial opportunities for eighteenth-century musicians were extremely limited, and only the very finest musicians, such as Handel, who was performing his *Messiah* in Dublin at approximately the same time that Pockrich arrived on the musical scene, could rely on their talent alone to bring in cash. The rest, like Pockrich, had to rely on gimmicks or hype. (For many female performers, this involved developing a deliberately "indecent" reputation to reel in the crowds.) The announcement for Pockrich's first concert, which appeared in *Faulkner's Dublin Journal* in the last week of April 1743, showcases the Captain's rhetorical gifts:

> At the Theatre in Smock-Alley, on Tuesday 3rd May, will be a musical Performance upon Glasses with other Instruments accompanied with Voices.... This being the first time that Glasses were ever introduced in Concert, it is hoped, that curiosity will induce the Town, to see what has so much surprised those who have heard them, even at the greatest

disadvantage . . . All Gentlemen that love a cheerful Glass, will undoubtedly be zealous in the Affair.

One rising member of the local Dublin music scene was a boy soprano named John Carteret Pilkington. Fourteen years old, Pilkington earned a paltry wage as a freelance verse writer for assorted magazines. Three different times, he and his mother were placed in Marshalsea prison, presumably for debt. Pilkington briefly tried his hand as a naval volunteer, but after a miserable week-long sea voyage, he returned to Dublin and sought his solace in a pub. It was here, after settling in to a night of drinking warm punch, that Pilkington first met Pockrich. The Captain cut quite a figure, Pilkington reported: he was tall, and wearing "a big wig and a sword."

As the two began chatting, Pilkington mentioned his recent singing performance at a concert in Cork. At this, Pockrich eagerly rose up, asking, "Why, can you sing?" When Pilkington said yes, Pockrich implored him to hum a tune. Pilkington happily obliged. When he finished, Pockrich exclaimed, "Bravo! Bravo! By God, I'll make your fortune."

With typical modesty, Pockrich then announced himself to be "perhaps the best master of harmony in the known world."

Already scheming to rope Pilkington in as a musical partner, Pockrich said he would give the boy an immediate demonstration of his genius. He pulled from his coat sixteen large pins, along with a small hammer. On a small round table, Pockrich hammered the pins into parallel rows, then pulled from his pocket two lengths of brass wire. "What tune will you have?" he demanded of the youth. When Pilkington said "The Black Joke," Pockrich told him to lay his ear to the table so he could "hear and admire." To Pilkington's astonishment, the older man then played the song "with all its variations," his musical contraption sounding much like a dulcimer.

Cheered by Pilkington's hearty applause, Pockrich laid out a series of drinking glasses, which he "tuned" by filling with different amounts of water. He then ran through a repertoire of many of the latest songs, his "elegant taste" giving the boy "delight and satisfaction." Having made his point, Pockrich laid out for Pilkington the scope of his plans. "I have at home glasses as large as bells of my own invention," he said, "that have a sound as loud as an organ, but more delicate and pleasing to the ear." Pockrich had named this invention the "Angelick Organ." "Now, Sir," he proposed to Pilkington, "as we are both gentlemen, and both possessed of excellence in the science of music, if we unite together, we must make a fortune." They would go on tour, with Pilkington the vocal attraction at Pockrich's concerts. The boy would receive £100 a year plus board and lodging.

Poor and desperate, Pilkington needed no encouragement to take the older man up on his offer. They left the pub and headed toward Pockrich's residence. (Ever shameless, and talking of their "future earnings," Pockrich "borrowed" from Pilkington the fare for the coach.) When they arrived at Pockrich's place in Bridestreet, the Captain explained that his current residence was the only place he could find where his music wouldn't bother his neighbors. Still, Pilkington was unprepared for the sight that greeted him once the light was struck: the most "litter'd dirty hole," the boy reported, "I had ever yet seen." The furniture was sparse: a cheap bed, a chair, a frame holding a number of large glasses, and a violincello case. Noting Pilkington's look of dismay, Pockrich tried to comfort him by saying that all "superfluous" furniture had been removed from the room, and that "he never suffered a servant to clean" the place, "lest their damn'd mops and brushes would break his glasses." He failed to mention that he'd blown his large inheritance on his failed plots, and was now living hand to mouth.

In a further attempt to reassure the boy, Pockrich sat down and played Handel's *Water Music* on his glasses, along with several other pieces. Pilkington agreed that the music "made some amends for the wretched appearance of every thing about him." Nor did the boy, steeped in poverty, have any other options.

Their partnership decided, the Captain and Pilkington rehearsed for the next two months. Once their repertoire was settled, Pockrich set up a gala concert at Tailor's Hall in Dublin. The streetcorners of the city were covered in advertisements for the event, while local newspapers sang the praises of the angelick organ. Concert tickets were distributed to the nobility. On the night of the event, Tailor's Hall was richly illuminated, catching the attention of passersby.

Three hours before the concert's kickoff, Pockrich set up and tuned his musical glasses. He then stepped out to grab some water. In his absence, disaster struck: a large female pig wandered into the room and knocked over the glasses, smashing Pockrich's angelick organ into "glittering fragments." According to Pilkington, "When the Captain returned, and found his lofty castles in the air reduced to an heap of rubbish, he looked just like Mark Anthony, when he beholds the body of Julius Caesar on the earth, and says: Oh! Mighty Caesar, dost thou lie so low?"

The Captain and his boy soprano saw their hopes for "a present and future subsistence" dashed.

There is no specific record of Pockrich and Pilkington performing together after that night, but Pockrich, for one, didn't let disaster keep him down. He rebuilt his angelick organ and continued to perform in public, including a show on March 1, 1744, at Mr. Hunt's Great Auction Room in London, and at least two shows at Tailor's with a first-time female vocalist, Miss Young, who sang, "Tell Me, lovely Shepherd."

One year later, Pockrich, a bachelor, married Margaret White. In true Captain-like fashion, the marriage was marked by error: each partner had assumed the other had money. Both were wrong. After running up sizable dress-related debts, Margaret White eloped from Dublin with an actor named Theophilus Cibber. Their union wasn't long for this world: not far from port, their Scotland-bound ship sank, killing everyone on board.

As for Pockrich, the highlight of his adventures with the angelick organ may have come when bailiffs arrived at his brewery near Islandbridge to haul him off to prison, must likely for outstanding debts.

"Gentlemen," Pockrich told them, "I am your prisoner, but

before I do myself the honor to attend you, give me leave as an humble performer of music, to entertain you with a tune."

"Sir," one of the bailiffs replied, "we come here to execute our warrant, not to hear tunes."

"Gentlemen," Pockrich said, "I submit to your authority, but in the interim, while you are only taking a dram, . . . Here, Jack," he called to his servant, "bring a bottle of the Ros Solis I lately distilled."

As the bailiffs sipped their drinks, Pockrich played a prelude on his glasses, then launched into a virtuosic performance of "The Black Joke." The bailiffs watched, quiet and still, as Pockrich wound through the song's turns and variations. When he finished, several seconds ticked by in silence.

Finally one of the bailiffs found his voice. "Sir," he told Pockrich, "upon your parole of honor to keep the secret, we give you your liberty." Having granted Pockrich reprieve, the bailiff said: "'Tis well, playing upon the glasses is not more common: if it were, I believe our trade would find little employment."

Pockrich continued to perform on his musical glasses in England and Ireland for the next fifteen years. In November 1759, in the midst of one of his tours, he was staying at Hamlin's Coffee House in London when a massive fire broke out, possibly in Pockrich's room, destroying the whole coffeehouse and several surrounding residences. The Captain and his angelick organ were no more.

Hearing about Pockrich's death, one of his detractors snidely remarked that he had blown his entire fortune without "ever even giving a good dinner." Others clearly found the Captain a charming character, however, as can be seen in this elegy from Brockhill Newburgh's *Essays*:

> *Old Pock, no more, still lives in deathless fame,*
> *He blazed when young, when old expired in flame,*
> *Mourn him, ye bogs, in tears discharge your tides:*
> *No more old Pock shall tap your spongy hides*
> *Ye geese, ye ganders, cackle doleful lays,*
> *No more his mountain tops your flocks shall graze.*
> *Be silent, dumb, ye late harmonious glasses:*
> *Free from surprise securely sleep ye lasses.*

Whether Pockrich knew it or not, his angelick organ was part of a long tradition of so-called musical glasses. It is not known when or where people first began using glass vessels as musical instruments, but the first mention of the practice dates from thirteenth-century China, where an instrument called the Shui Chan was made up of "nine cups, struck with a stick." A Japanese contemporary of that instrument, described as "a teacup-shaped porcelain gong," is also on record. Thirteenth-century Persians knew of the musical glasses, too, which in this case took the form of earthenware bowls filled with varying amounts of water, and which may date from an even earlier period. Two centuries later, an Arabic writer referred to a water-filled set of musical cups and jars.

By the 1700s, this antique form of music making was well known to Europeans, likely due to fifteenth- and sixteenth-century travelers and adventurers who had traversed the east. In the 1600s a book titled *The Voyages and Travels of the Ambassadors from the Duke of Holstein to the Great Duke of Muscovy and the King of Persia* appeared in England, France, Germany, and Holland. One passage describes an evening's entertainment in Persia, where an instrument called the tamera, similar to a lute, is accompanied by "seven porcelane cups, full of water," which are struck by "two little sticks."

A. Hyatt King traces the first reference to European musical glasses to Franchino Gafori's *Theorica Musicae*, published in Milan in 1492, the year of Columbus's first voyage to America.

The book features a woodcut of what is apparently a Pythagorean experiment in which one person uses sticks to tap on glasses of varying amounts of water, while a man behind him taps on bells to match the sounds. Music was at the heart of Pythagorean principles due to its alleged ability to calm the nerves. More than 150 years later, a German work, *Deliciae Physico-mathematicae*, included a section on how to make "a cheerful wine-music" by filling glasses with different amounts of wine and rubbing a wet finger around their rims. The book says that the same effect can be gained with brandy and water. Going one step beyond the Pythagorean concepts, it argues that glass music can have a healing effect on not just emotional but also physical ailments. (The healing powers attributed to glass music become especially relevant in the later history of the glass armonica.)

In 1627, Francis Bacon wrote about making water in a wineglass "frisk" by rubbing a wet finger around the rim, although he made no mention of the sound that is produced. Eleven years later, Galileo gave a more explicit treatment of this same phenomenon in *Two New Sciences*, his final book. That Galileo would be attuned to glass's musical properties is perhaps not surprising: his father, Vincenzo, was a renowned musician and music theorist, who taught his son how to play and compose for

A woodcut from Franchino Gafori's
Theorica Musicae, 1492.

the lute. Among other things, Galileo's father made pioneering discoveries regarding the measurement of octaves, overturning centuries of conventional musical theory in the process.

Galileo wrote *Two New Sciences* under the worst of conditions: the Vatican had placed him under house arrest, his health was weak and his eyesight fading, and he was devastated by the recent death of his daughter Maria. Because the Vatican had forbidden him from writing about astronomy—nor was he allowed to publish anything, on *any* subject, though he undertook extraordinary measures to ensure that his work would see the light of day—Galileo wrote instead about his three decades of experimentation in physics. In the process, he engaged in groundbreaking pure mathematics, the likes of which hadn't been seen in over two millennia.

Yet in the midst of this mathematical flurry, and despite his miserable state, Galileo made a lengthy detour into the musical sounds that can be drawn from glasses. Noting that "a glass of water may be made to emit a tone merely by the friction of the finger-tip upon the rim of the glass," Galileo went on for several pages to discuss the technical particulars of this phenomenon, and their relationship to experiments with pendulums.

Thirty-five years later, the Jesuit scholar and polymath

Athanasius Kircher, often called "the last Renaissance man" or "the last man to know everything," wrote of his own experiments with the wet-finger-around-the-wineglass phenomenon. The author of dozens of books on every possible subject, from Egyptology to geology to microbes to the magic lantern, Kircher also invented the megaphone and the magnetic clock. In one of his later books, the *Phonurgia Nova*, Kircher tackled the ways in which music influences human beings, and the mathematics and physics of how sound is propagated in enclosed spaces. The book describes an experiment in which one takes a "glass drinking vessel of any size" and fills it with water. If, after doing this, Kircher writes, "you wet your index finger and rub the outer lip of the vessel in a circular movement," you will "perceive an extraordinary sort of sound resembling ringing metal."

The first European mention of musical glasses as a concert instrument may be in Walther's *Musicalishes Lexicon*, published in 1732. The author uses the French term "vérillon" when describing the concerto glasses played by Silesian native Christian Gottfried Helmond. An instructional booklet published six years later provides a basic outline of how to make a vérillon: based on the booklet's illustration, the unwieldy instrument consisted of eighteen water-filled glasses placed in a row on a narrow-ended board. The player used thin sticks to tap the sides of the glasses. According to the booklet, the vérillon was often used for ceremonial purposes, such as the musical portion of church liturgy. It is not clear why sticks were still used to play the glasses, given that people knew at the time that rubbing the rims with a wet finger produced a sweeter, longer lasting tone.

Richard Pockrich's angelick organ, then, was really an updated vérillon, one that he eventually took to playing with his fingers instead of two sticks. But whatever the originality of Pockrich's creation, his is the name that Benjamin Franklin cited years later in describing the origins of his own musical invention.

Any "musical glass" or "singing glass"—that is, a glass capable of producing a tone—is really a glass bell, and it operates on the same principle as a traditional metal bell. The particular tone a glass produces depends on how thin the glass is (the glass must be thin enough to vibrate). Striking or tapping a glass—for example, a wineglass—drives energy into its bell, causing it to vibrate at its particular frequency. Rubbing the rim of a glass with a wet finger produces the same effect as a violin bow scraping a string. The finger briefly attaches to the rim and twists the glass until it slips, whereby the finger catches it again. This process occurs hundreds or thousands of times a second, which, again, drives energy into the bell, causing it to vibrate. A glass's pitch can be lowered by pouring water into the bell.

Of course, thin glass produces extra risks for players of the musical glasses. Dropping the glasses isn't the only hazard—loud sounds can also shatter them (though this is less common with today's high-quality glass). The Jewish Talmud includes laws based on this phenomenon: "When a cock shall stretch forth its neck into the hollow of a glass vessel and sing therein in such a way as to break it," reads one, "the full loss shall be paid." States another law: "When a horse neighs or an ass brays and so breaks a glass vessel, the half of the loss shall be paid."

If Richard Pockrich gave us the direct forebear of Franklin's glass armonica, the first famous performer on the musical glasses in eighteenth-century London was a wellborn woman named Ann Ford, the daughter of a prominent lawyer, and the niece, on her mother's side, of the queen's personal physician. A musical prodigy, Ann wrote the first handbook on how to play the musical glasses, and she was a star performer and composer on the viola da gamba, among other instruments, as well.

A doted-upon only child, Ann received an expensive (and

Ann Ford playing the viola da gamba.

rare) education, and she displayed an early gift for arts, dancing, and foreign languages. It was clear from the start, however, that her talent for music outshone all her other gifts: accordingly, she received her musical training from "the most eminent professors of the day." She seems to have held a special fondness for uncommon instruments. By her late teens she was an expert player of the wire-strung English guitar and the gut-strung Spanish guitar, rarities at the time, and the viola da gamba, which was no longer in popular use. On Sundays she gave concerts, well attended by the high society, which "attracted the notice of all the gay and fashionable world." Often she was accompanied by renowned violinists, cellists, and harpsichord players—the composer Thomas Arne was one—and singers such as the legendary castrato Giusto Tenducci.

In addition to her instrumental expertise, Ann possessed by all accounts a remarkable singing voice, as can be seen in the testimony of an attendee at an October 1758 production of *Julius Caesar*:

> They introduced a procession of vestals to mourn over Caesar's body.... One of them sang a dirge divinely well. She is, I think ... the most pleasing singer I ever heard. I don't dare say

the best because I have not judgment enough to decide, but I know that I would rather hear her than any Italian I have yet heard. She is a Miss Ford, daughter of a sort of Lawyer in the city.

Not long after this performance, Ann's father, Thomas Ford, decided it was time for his cherished offspring to be betrothed to a respectable gentleman. To the free-spirited Ann, this prospect was unbearable, and she fled from her father's house to hide at the residence of her wealthy friend Elizabeth Thicknesse. But if she thought she was safe, she was sorely mistaken. The premises were soon surrounded by the police of the fearsome Bow Street magistrate Sir John Fielding, who had signed a warrant for her arrest. Fielding's men grabbed Ann and placed her in a carriage to transport her home to the paternal hearth.

Riding next to Ann in the carriage was a familiar gentleman who had long made clear his attraction to her. He told her he loved her and wished to be her husband, but Ann firmly rejected him, being in no mood to become anyone's wife. Her father, however, greatly approved of the gentleman as a suitor, and assured Ann that she and the gentleman would enjoy a happy married life among the man's substantial estates in Jamaica.

This was too much for Ann's strong, independent sensibilities. Once again she took flight from her father's mansion, installing herself in a residence at Kensington, where she successfully avoided her pursuers. Rather than bemoan her situation, she decided to enlist her musical talents to render herself finally free of her father's influence. Being well acquainted with the English nobility, Ann developed a plan to enlist their benefaction for her music. She rented the Opera House for a three-night stand in March and April 1760, and, with a group of performers, prepared a musical recital. Tickets for the concerts were in high demand: According to one account, "every one was eager to subscribe; and the young performer was wooed, like Danae of old, in a shower of gold."

The bold, even outrageous nature of Ann's plan is striking: as William Zeitler observes, "hers were the only subscription concerts held in London between 1756 and 1763." Ann's musical talents weren't the only appeal, as the large and "fashionable" audiences were "perhaps more attracted by the scandal than the music." Her embarrassed father offered her a regular salary to desist from her public musical life, but she refused his entreaties.

Angered by his daughter's rebelliousness, and scandalized by the thought of her appearing onstage—on *any* stage—her father again called upon magistrate Sir John Fielding, who dispatched his officers to the theater in the Haymarket. On the way, however, they were blocked by Lord Tankerville, a Royal Guard officer, who declared that anyone who tried to disrupt the concert would be punished. Members of the royal family were expected to attend the show, Tankerville told Fielding's men, and he would call out a full detachment of horse-mounted troops to fend off anyone who tried to stop Miss Ford.

Ann herself felt a bit jittery as she huddled backstage in white satin and pearls on opening night. To calm her stagefright, Prince Edward drank a cup of tea with her. Then the prince's attendant took Ann by the hand and led her to the stage, where she was greeted with a hearty round of applause. She began her opening number, one of Handel's oratorios, with the lines, "Return, O God of Hosts/Relieve thy servant in distress!" Her voice was so beautiful, her emotions so "exquisite," that several of her friends "burst into tears."

After the performances, exhausted by the stress of the scandal, Ann decamped for Bath, where she hoped to take refuge. While in Bath, she socialized with the portrait and landscape painter Thomas Gainsborough, who was seeking fashionable clientele to establish his studio. In a move designed to attract attention, Gainsborough painted an arresting, full-sized portrait of Ann that he displayed in his painting room. By far the grandest project of his career to that point, Gainsborough's portrait of Ann achieved the painter's goal of drawing in potential clientele, while also furthering Ann's reputation as a remarkable, but slightly outrageous, woman. A female visitor to Gainsborough's studio in October 1760 expressed the common sentiment: "Miss Ford's picture, a whole length with her guitar, [shows] a most extraordinary figure, handsome and bold; but I should be very sorry to have any one I loved set forth in such a manner." As Zeitler notes, the painting was, for its time and place, "borderline risqué." Joseph Burke writes of how, in the picture, Ann "crosses her legs above the knee, a masculine freedom" that is absent in the portraits of women by Van Dyck and Rubens. "An air of high breeding," Burke suggests, "redeems the suggestion of wantonness in the bold asymmetrical pose."

After nine months in Bath, Ann began the year 1761 by putting on two more concerts at the Haymarket in London. It may be that the months of scandal had taken their toll on Ann's popularity (and her spirit), because this time she was performing alone, and the advertisements stated that the shows would be "the last time of her appearing in Public." And while

Portrait of Ann Ford by Thomas Gainsborough.

the events were intended to be part of a subscription series, the lack of further concerts that year suggests that the plan had to be scrapped for lack of interest. That fall, Ann made another attempt at a concert series, this time in Cox's Auction House, a much less reputable venue than the Haymarket (though the advertisements stressed that the room would be heated). Her ticket prices had also been slashed by three quarters.

This time, Ann took care to emphasize that, as part of her repertoire, she would be performing on the musical glasses. A count who attended her November 7 concert reported that Ann, "a pupil of Schumann . . . has performed here for some time on musical glasses. She plays entire concerts with one finger, on a row of tuned wine-glasses . . . and gives her audience a varied entertainment." The teacher to whom the count referred was the German composer Frederic Schumann, and he was a popular instructor of both the musical glasses and the English guitar.

Ann's concerts at the Auction House were her last public performances, save for a benefit concert for a pauper's hospital decades later. They occurred at a time of mounting competition, in which London witnessed an explosion of "daily exhibition performances given by young ladies and by self-publicising teachers." To attract the public's increasingly divided attention, many of these performers, like Ann and her teacher, Schumann, played unusual instruments like the musical glasses. Schumann may have actually been irritated by his pupil's concerts at the Auction House, for he mounted a competing series at his Bury Street house, declaring that he would play music "every Day upon the GLASSES, between the Hours of One and Three."

On November 2, 1761, five days before her final performance, Ann published *Instructions for Playing on the Musical Glasses*, the very first "method book" for mastering the instrument. (One can imagine Schumann's displeasure at this occurrence, as well.) She begins the book with a grand statement of the glasses' uniqueness, and a heady prediction of the instrument's shining future:

> As the Tones of the Musical Glasses are, from their Similitude, more like the human Voice, than any musical Instrument, that ever was, or perhaps ever will be invented: there is much Reason to suppose, these Glasses will, in a short Time, become as common a piece of Furniture as an Harpsichord: and that every Lady, who can play or sing (but more particularly the latter) will be furnished with an instrument.

Ann proves a clever and inspired player of the instrument. She suggests tipping a glass in order to shift the water level and modify the tonal pitch. She also provides a meticulous account of how to achieve the most sonorous tones. After rubbing one's fingers with the "Pulp of an unripe Gripe [sic]," Ann writes, one traces a circular motion around the glass's rim. Not only is the tone of the musical glasses "superior to every other Instrument," she declares, it is perhaps "the only one from which you hear the Effect without Cause."

Shortly after the book's publication, Ann left London to assist her old friend Elizabeth Thicknesse with the birth of her sixth child. The baby was born healthy in January 1762, but a scant three months later, tragedy struck: Lady Elizabeth died, leaving her husband, Phillip, with a brood of three daughters and three sons. Deeply distraught at the loss of his wife, Lord Thicknesse placed his offspring into Ann's care and retreated into privacy to mourn. When at long last his grief abated, and he returned to his family, Lord Thicknesse began to think that the best replacement for his late wife, Elizabeth, might be her oldest and closest friend. On September 27 of that year, Ann Ford became Ann Thicknesse, the Lord's third (and final) wife. Aged forty-three, the Lord was eighteen years Ann's senior. He was also, Zeitler writes, "notorious as an ardent supporter of the slave trade, a blackmailer, a lecher and a sadist." Whether due to Lord Thicknesse's reputation or not, Ann's father boycotted the wedding.

Regardless of the enmity her husband engendered among many locals, Ann's standing as an "elegant, delicate, powerful woman"—now thankfully past her days of scandal—remained unsullied throughout the rest of her life. Though her public performances were behind her, Ann continued to be a highly regarded musician, and a vocalist of rare skill. In 1806, fourteen years after her husband, Phillip, died in her arms, and decades after her time on London's musical stage, the sixty-eight-year-old Ann continued to be described as "in many respects the most singular, and if it may be added, perhaps the most accomplished woman of her day." After spending her last years living with her close friend Sarah Cooper, Ann died in January 1824 at the ripe old age of eighty-six.

2

BENJAMIN FRANKLIN
AND MUSIC

Throughout his long life, Benjamin Franklin possessed a deep and enduring interest in music. He was a capable player of several musical instruments: In addition to the glass armonica, he played the harpsichord, the viola da gamba, and the musical bells, and he carried with him a small dulcimer-type instrument called a sticcado at all times. He also loved to sing and write lyrics, at one point even composing a string quartet. Music was a constant companion wherever Franklin lived: in Philadelphia's meeting houses, he sang rounds with his friends in the Junto, while, at home on Market Street with his family, he loved nothing more than performing duets with his daughter, Sally. In England, where he joined a "little musical club," he heard Handel's latest compositions (including a charity performance of the *Messiah* a mere two weeks after the composer's death), and he regularly attended fashionable operas and concerts. In France he delighted in musical gatherings at the homes of his close friends Madame Brillon and Madame Helvétius, where, in addition to singing with his companions, he mingled with some of Paris's foremost musical talents, and heard the very best cellists, flautists, horn players, and keyboardists. In one instance his love of music almost caused his death: in 1781, he narrowly escaped a quick-moving fire at the Paris opera house. Franklin's passion for music didn't attach itself to those who performed it, however. Like most colonists, he thought professional musicians were social parasites. He derided the "fiddling man" whose labor brought forth no concrete goods.

Part of Franklin's approach to music was intellectual. He was interested in music's power and scope, the range of effects that it had on its listeners. As a scientist, he wanted to know the particulars of music's properties, and why they were so appealing to the ear. Yet music, for Franklin, was also much more than an analytical concern. As Ellen Cohn writes, Franklin believed music "existed in a social context" and that "its essence was communication." Music united people; it moved them emotionally, and even contained an abstract wisdom. Those who played instruments together or traded verses in a song were connected as *friends*, a notion of the greatest import to the highly social Franklin, who collected friends by the dozens wherever he lived. For this reason, his preferred locale for music was the "home or tavern," and his favorite melodies were those of the "common people," the simple Scottish tunes that had been passed down through the oral tradition. He attended many highbrow concerts at Europe's grandest halls, and he was a sophisticated listener and critic, but it was the unadorned Scottish songs, heartrending or bawdy, satirical or nakedly emotional, that captured his heart. He referred to them in letters, and discussed and sang them for hours with friends. He was even inspired to pen a number of his own compositions.

The Franklin family's gift for music ran across generations. Franklin's father, Josiah, the clan's patriarch, had a highly regarded singing voice, which he complemented with his proficiency on the violin. (Josiah's preferred tunes were hymns.) Franklin's daughter, Sally, was musically gifted as well, a trait that her father took great pains to cultivate, buying her a fine harpsichord and hand-selecting a first-rate tutor. Even when he was living in Europe, an ocean away from Sally, Franklin spent hours seeking out quality music to send her at home.

Sally wasn't the only younger family member whose musical talent and education Franklin encouraged. His great-nephew Josiah Williams was an up-and-coming harpsichord player who dreamed of studying with London's legendary music teacher John Stanley. Stanley, it happened, was an old friend of Franklin's: More than a decade earlier, he had guided Franklin's purchase of Sally's harpsichord, and he'd recommended the best music to shape her education. Now, in 1770, Stanley, retired from teaching, granted Franklin another musical favor. With Stanley's blessing, Josiah Williams traveled from Pennsylvania to London, where he roomed with his great-uncle and spent the next two years—the last of his life, it turned out—as Stanley's lone and final student.

For an eighteenth-century male of Franklin's social stature, there remained a fine distinction between "gentleman amateur" and actual musician, no matter how skilled a player that gentleman might be. The same held true for Franklin's musically gifted peers Thomas Jefferson, Patrick Henry, and Francis Hopkinson. No matter how dearly Franklin loved to play his glass armonica, he could never do so in a context that implied he was receiving pay for his performance. Only servants and slaves were allowed to play at public congregations. In fact, advertisements for slaves in such newspapers as the *Virginia Gazette* often specified musical talent as a qualification.

Part of Franklin's investigation of the essence of music's "soul" involved determining the passions and sentiments that music could evoke. Inspired by his friend André Morellet's argument that music was "a metaphorical language capable of depicting both physical objects and human emotions," Franklin compiled a list, nearly fifty items long, of music's emotional palette:

> Desire, joy, grief, complaint, expostulation, resignation, patience, boldness or courage, resolution & firmness or fortitude, anger, rashness, contempt, peevishness & quarrelsomeness, tranquility & composure of mind, consolation, pity, tenderness, fondness, reverence or veneration, resentment, courtesy, magnanimity, regret, meekness, satisfaction, triumph, insolence, caution, diffidence, fear, prudence, terror, distraction of mind, delicacy, indifference, yielding, obstinacy, moderation, condescension, frankness, gravity, moroseness, pride, sullenness, presumption.

Still, for all of Franklin's musical sensitivity, sophistication, and intelligence, he never wavered in his belief that traditional

Scottish folk songs represented the world's finest music. In fact, he showed an active and lifelong *dislike* for the complex, high-art Baroque and Classical music that filled eighteenth-century Europe's fanciest halls. Franklin felt this contemporary music was the equivalent to "the pleasure derived from watching acrobats execute difficult stunts," that it was "contrived." Old Scottish tunes, on the other hand, had an organic beauty that was both timeless and universally appealing. They were heartfelt, unpretentious, and therefore pure. This was of a piece with Franklin's passion for simplicity and his veneration of the plainspoken man. True to his nature, Franklin had approached the matter scientifically, by closely observing the facial expressions of London's concertgoers as they listened to various pieces of music. Traditional Scottish melodies, he determined, produced the expressions of greatest joy.

British writers of the time, reaching back to classical roots, also fetishized simplicity as a musical and artistic objective. Music's primary purpose was to "reach the heart." This idea wasn't new, but it received renewed and increased attention as an "age of sensibility" marked the second half of the eighteenth century. The philosopher Jean-Jacques Rousseau set the agenda with his 1752 opera *Le Devin du Village*, in which, with a spare melodicism, he contrasted the innocence of rural life with the city's rank corruption. British composers such as Charles Avison took up the call, proclaiming that "a pompous Display of Art will destroy its own Intentions: on which Account, one of the best general Rules, perhaps, that can be given for musical Expression, is . . . *an unaffected Strain of Nature and Simplicity.*" Pathos ruled the day. As James Beattie wrote in his 1762 essay on music, "All popular and favourite airs; all that remains of the old national music in every country; all military marches, church-tunes, and other compositions that are . . . addressed to the heart . . . are remarkable for simplicity."

In a letter to his royal friend Lord Kames, who had written that "all music is resolvable into melody and harmony," Franklin offered this affable but subtle rebuke: "The reason why Scottish tunes have lived so long and will probably live forever—if they escape being stifled in modern affected ornament—is merely this: that they are really Compositions of melody and harmony united, or rather that their melody *is* harmony." The reason is built into the music's structure, which centers on the notes most pleasing to the ear: the tonic, third, fifth, and octave. We can't *help*, Franklin felt, but find the music harmonious. It was music fit for the heavens. Flirting with his French friend Madame

Brillon, he imagined that in the afterlife, when they were finally a couple, they would be serenaded by harp-playing angels strumming their beloved Scottish tunes.

As Cohn writes, Franklin's love of these songs "had a functional as well as an aesthetic component." We can see this in an exchange he had with his older brother Peter, who, having written the lyrics to a new ballad, requested his help in procuring a composer. Instead, Franklin criticized Peter's employment of a nontraditional meter. Peter's effort to be modern, Franklin felt, had harmed the ballad's chances of success. Instead, Peter should have molded his words to a familiar tune. If he had done so, he could have "given it to some country girl in the heart of Massachusetts, who has never heard any other than . . . old simple ditties, but has a naturally good ear, [and] she might more probably have made a pleasing popular tune for you, than any of our masters here." Peter needed to recognize that songs form "a melodious way of speaking," and that, just as plain language is most effective for making a point, melody and lyrics hewn closely together have the greatest impact. Franklin ended his letter by poking fun at Handel, the most fashionable of London's modern composers. The virtuosity of Handel's *Judas Maccabaeus*, Franklin wrote, completely overwhelmed the text. Among the oratorio's many "defects" were "drawling," "stuttering," and "screaming without cause."

Franklin followed his own advice in the songs he composed. He placed the lyrics he wrote on top of classic melodies, a common practice of the day. There was no need for musical notation; any listener of the time would have known the tunes. More impressive is the lyrical, tonal, and formal variety Franklin exhibited in his small body of work. Like their author, Franklin's musical corpus ranges from amusing to risqué, from traditional to politically pointed. He attempted both gentle ballads and hearty chorus tunes.

Franklin wrote his first two published songs—lyrics, really—at age thirteen, when he was an apprentice to his printer brother, James. Both were ballads that covered recent, heavily publicized, occurrences: the drowning of an entire family in one, and the killing of Blackbeard the pirate in the other. James printed copies of the lyrics, which Franklin peddled on the streets of Boston. Due to their sensational nature, and their focus on current events, both sold briskly. Barely into his teens, Franklin's commercial acumen was already apparent. Regardless, his no-nonsense father, Josiah, discouraged any further attempts at verse.

Franklin wrote several more songs over the course of his lifetime, with the most intriguing of them reflecting his political sentiments. Around 1765, Franklin penned a tune titled "The Mother Country" that showed, even at this relatively late date, his then commitment to the British Crown despite its loutish behavior:

> Her Orders so odd are, we often suspect
> That Age has impaired her sound Intellect:
> But still an old Mother should have due Respect,
> Which nobody can deny, &c.
>
> . . .
>
> Know too, ye bad Neighbours, who aim to divide
> The Sons from the Mother, that still she's our Pride;
> And if ye attack her we're all of her side,
> Which nobody can deny, &c.

In 1775, his commitment to "mother" now shattered, and the Revolution under way, Franklin poured his politics into another song, "The King's Own Regulars; and Their Triumphs over the Irregulars," a caustic attack on the British Army:

As they could not get before us, how could they look us in the
face?
We took care they should not, by scampering away apace;
That they had not much to brag of, is a very plain case.
For if they beat us in the fight, we beat them in the race.

Not all of Franklin's songs were weighty. He wrote drinking songs and comic songs, as well as a paean to his wife, Deborah, titled "My Plain Country Joan." He meant all of his tunes to be sung communally, by roaring hearths in local taverns, or in the comfortable sitting rooms of one's closest friends. Franklin's songs are a vivid expression of his convivial nature, and his lifelong devotion to clarity and simplicity. Even into his last months, he continued to rail, in a letter to his sister Jane, against "the complex Music, of late, in my Opinion, too much in vogue, it being only pleasing to learned Ears, who can be delighted with the Difficulty of Execution, instead of simple Harmony and Melody."

When he wrote those words Franklin was mostly bedridden, taking opium to quell the pains of age. Though Jane had hoped to see her brother in person after his long sojourn overseas, it was not to be. Rather, as they had done for decades, the siblings poured their feelings into their correspondence.

"It seems a long time since I heard from you," Jane confided to Franklin. "But I had the Pleasure in a Dream Last night to hear you Play a delightful Tune on the Harpsicord."

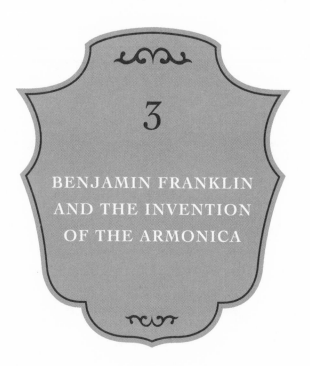

3

BENJAMIN FRANKLIN
AND THE INVENTION
OF THE ARMONICA

In the decades before the American
Revolution, Pennsylvania was a proprietary colony, meaning that
it was ruled by an individual family—in this case, the Penns—as
opposed to royal or elected officials. Most of the colonies began
this way, but by the 1720s the majority had been converted into
royal colonies instead. Pennsylvania, however, along with Mary-
land and Delaware, was ruled by proprietors until the Revolution broke out.

Benjamin Franklin was a member of the Pennsylvania Assembly, and still dedicated to the Crown, when fissures between
the colonists and the Penns (and the Penns' political minions)
first appeared in the 1750s. Two related issues drove the Penns'
approach to colonial rule: they wanted to spend as little money

as possible, and they wanted their land to remain tax-free. These desires were at odds with the colony's financial needs. Franklin, though a loyal "Briton," grew increasingly angered at the Penns' refusal to cede any control of Pennsylvania's governance and taxation to the colonists.

By 1756, the tensions between the colonists and the proprietors had come to a head. The Assembly decided to confront the Penns directly about their denial of the colony's right to govern itself. As the New Year tolled, the Assembly elected to send Franklin to London to lobby on the colony's behalf. First he would petition Thomas Penn to give the Assembly greater control over taxation and related functions. If Penn refused his entreaties, Franklin would take the colony's case to Parliament.

At the time of Franklin's arrival in 1757, London was a metropolis of 750,000 people—a far cry from the meager 23,000 inhabitants of Philadelphia, at the time America's largest city. Filth, crime, crowding, and rigid class divisions defined the daily experience of London's residents. But in the midst of this reality, the city also contained a liveliness and worldliness that manifested among the increasing numbers of writers, artists, intellectuals, and scientists who frequented the city's hundreds of coffeehouses. A budding class of shopkeepers, businessmen, and entrepreneurs fueled the city's energies as well.

Franklin was already well known in England, thanks in part to his earlier election to the Royal Society, which had guaranteed an international audience for his groundbreaking research on electricity. He'd also received honorary degrees from Oxford and St. Andrews; respectful Londoners always greeted him as "Dr. Franklin." With his natural antipathy toward the idle aristocracy, Franklin found a quick home among the middle-class thinkers and doers who were driving the city's extraordinary growth. His new friends were printers, journalists, merchants, philosophers, scientists, physicians, and professors, that stratum of society who formed discussion groups in coffeehouses and devoured the numerous periodicals that coffeehouse owners provided to their patrons. Politics, science, business: these were subjects that aroused Franklin's passions, and he found a rich cohort of like-minded colleagues in the British Empire's capital city.

But it would be inaccurate to say that he was occupied wholly with serious (or, rather, nonartistic) matters. In keeping with his passion for music, Franklin was a dedicated concertgoer in England. At the time, London offered probably the greatest range and quantity of concert life in Europe, with thousands of public concerts, some advertised and some not, taking place in music halls, ancient-music societies, and pleasure gardens throughout the city. Private concerts at personal residences remained popular, too.

Perhaps the most significant concert of Franklin's life occurred around 1761, when he watched his friend Edward Delaval perform on the musical glasses. Delaval came from a well-established Northumberland family: he was a man of science, a chemist and electrician, as well as a classical scholar and linguist, and a known figure in experimental psychology. A fellow at Cambridge University, Delaval was later elected a fellow of the Royal Society with Franklin's assistance. Years later he joined Franklin on a Royal Society committee tasked with determining how St. Paul's Cathedral might be shielded from lightning strikes.

Delaval the Loud, as his friends called him—he had a booming voice—was a regular performer on the musical glasses, owning one of the largest sets in the country. Delaval's musical skill, as well as the special (and spectral) qualities of the instrument, are attested to in this letter by Thomas Gray describing a Cambridge performance in 1760: "We heard Delaval the other night play upon the water glasses, & I was astonished. No instrument that I know has so celestial a tone. I thought it was a cherubim in a box." In another letter Gray writes that Delaval possesses "a charming set of glasses that sing like nightingales, & we have concerts every other night."

Franklin's attendance at one of Delaval's concerts provided his first exposure to the ethereal harmonies of glass-based music. He quickly declared himself "charmed with the sweetness" of the instrument's tones, "and the music produced from it." Still, in typical Franklin fashion, he saw room for improvement in the instrument's design. As he told his friend and frequent correspondent Giambattista Beccaria, a professor of experimental physics in Turin, Italy, and an early and ardent supporter of Franklin's electrical experiments, he desired "to see the glasses disposed in more convenient form, and brought together in a narrower compass, so as to admit a greater number of tones, and all within reach of hand to a person sitting before the instrument."

As historian H. W. Brands writes, "Franklin's genius generally consisted in observing commonplace phenomena and applying the principles behind them in a novel or peculiarly productive way." His ravenous curiosity made the world, for Franklin, an endlessly fascinating place. A key component of that curiosity was the constant drive to know *why*—why things worked one way and not another—and, equally importantly, whether there might be a better, faster, easier, more effective, or more useful way for that thing to work. His astonishing list of inventions and discoveries stems from that life-defining inquisitiveness. He wasn't out for riches—indeed, he refused to patent any of his inventions, believing instead that they were civic contributions, objects to be used for the public good. "As we enjoy great Advantages from the Inventions of others," he wrote, "we should be glad of an Opportunity to serve others by any Invention of ours, and this we should do freely and generously." Always, for Franklin, that drive to be *useful*, to focus one's energies on the betterment of society. His intense practicality, for which generations of Romantic-minded intellectuals mocked and dismissed him, was tied inextricably to this unyielding belief in the power and importance of civic virtue.

Franklin's cleverness, his inventiveness and intelligence, shone through even in his childhood days in Boston, where he and his friends whiled away hot summer days in the cooling waters of the Charles. Searching for a way to swim faster, Franklin realized that the relatively small size of human hands and feet limited the rate at which people could propel themselves through the water. To compensate, he built two oval paddles for his hands, and attached flippers—"a kind of sandals," he wrote—to his feet. With these, he sped himself easily past his floundering playmates. Another day, lazing by a mill pond, Franklin tied a kite around his bare waist, lay back in the water, and let the kite do its work. "Having then engaged another boy to carry my clothes round the pond," he recalled, "I began to cross the pond with my kite, which carried me quite over without the least fatigue and with the greatest pleasure imaginable."

Franklin's resourcefulness, and his seemingly boundless sense of wonder, were joined to a willingness—a compulsion, really, an almost tactile *need*—to interrogate the million mysteries, large and small, of the natural world through which he moved. These unknowns, these profound if alluring gaps in humankind's scientific (never mind theological) comprehension, were as entrancing as they were never ending. Franklin's lifelong attempts to unravel them, and to fill them in, led him, brilliant though untrained scientist that he was, to operate in the world as if it was his joyous laboratory, as bountiful in its curiosities as it was in its intellectual rewards. "For a new appearance," he wrote, "if it cannot be explain'd by our old principles, may afford us new ones, of use perhaps in explaining some other obscure parts of natural knowledge." Many of Franklin's celebrated inventions originated from the space where this radical inquisitiveness bound itself to his famed (sometimes celebrated, sometimes reviled) practicality.

The glass armonica, H. W. Brands notes, "fit the pattern" of Franklin's previous inventions. Up until now the musical glasses had been just that: a set of drinking glasses of varying sizes arranged on a table or stand and filled with water, which the performer played by rubbing his or her fingers around the rims. This arrangement was time-consuming, unreliable, and overly fragile.

In his quest to refine the instrument, Franklin undertook a series of experiments to improve its form. A doctor who visited him in May 1761 reported that "the electric genius" had constructed a dulcimer made of glass bells that "warble[d] like the sound of an organ." By the end of that year, Franklin had hit upon a novel and ingenious solution: he placed a series of thirty-seven glasses, from three to nine inches in diameter, on an iron spindle mounted flat in a wooden case. The performer sat on a bench and rotated the spindle by means of a foot pedal. Like a harpsichord, the instrument was played with two hands, meaning all ten fingers could be used at once—a much fuller sound than the musical glasses had previously allowed. In another innovation, each glass was ground to a specific note, which meant that no water was needed (though the performer's fingers had to be wet). In his letter to Beccaria, Franklin set down specific guidelines regarding the blowing of the glasses, the manner in which they should be tuned, and a tonal range of three octaves. As E. Power Biggs declares, these "radical" improvements "transformed the instrument."

Franklin went into exhaustive detail for Beccaria about how to construct the glass armonica, providing exact measurements of everything from the varying thickness of the glasses to the iron spindle, from the mahogany wheel to the case that holds the instrument. He specified the delicate process by which the glasses are fixed on the spindle and placed one inside the other. He also recommended marking the glasses to differentiate them. Franklin painted the insides of his own instrument's glasses: each semitone was white, while the octave's other notes featured "the seven prismatic colors, viz. C, red; D, orange; E, yellow; F, green; G, blue; A, indigo; B, purple; and C, red again." In this manner, the "glasses of the same colour (the white excepted) are always octaves to each other." (Franklin did not invent this particular sequence of colors and related notes. Isaac Newton, fifty years earlier, had related this same sequence, while Athanasius

Kircher, in his 1650 book *Musurgia Universalis*, expounded upon the relationship between sound and color.)

Having outlined for Beccaria the armonica's intricate design, Franklin moved on to the larger picture. "The advantages of this instrument," he wrote with unabashed enthusiasm, "are, that its tones are incomparably sweet beyond those of any other; that they may be swelled and softened at pleasure by stronger or weaker pressure of the finger, and continued to any length; and that the instrument, being once well tuned, never again wants tuning." Part of the instrument's unique sound, its often remarked upon "ethereal" quality, stems from how humans identify and pinpoint sounds, and how we locate them in the left or right ears. The armonica's primary timbre, pitched between 1,000 and 4,000 hertz, is located directly in the brain's "weak spot," the sound range where the brain has trouble identifying where the sound is coming from and what is producing it.

In a later letter, Franklin gave detailed instructions for how to play the armonica, and, more specifically, how to draw out the best tones from the glasses. The glasses themselves must be kept perfectly clean at all times, he wrote, without a hint of grease on them, including from the natural grease of the hands. Touching the glasses without washing one's hands first with soap was not allowed. Players also needed to keep a bottle of rainwater next to the instrument—spring water was "generally too hard" and produced a "harsh tone"—along with a sponge in a water-filled bowl. Next to that should be a teacup filled with grit-free chalk.

Before playing, one needed to soak one's fingers by pressing them hard on the sponge. Players then had to draw the moist sponge across all thirty-seven glasses while pumping the foot treadle, so that each glass was made slightly wet. Any nearby open windows or curtains should be shut or drawn, or the water on the glasses would too quickly dry.

If these directions were heeded, Franklin wrote, the armonica's tones would "come forth finely with the slightest Pressure of the Fingers imaginable," and could be swelled at leisure by simply increasing the pressure. If the tones grew less "smooth and soft" after a few minutes, players could simply dip the tips of their wet fingers into the chalk and rub it into their skin.

To build an instrument as complex as the armonica, Franklin needed to find craftsmen of the highest skill. This also fit the pattern of his earlier inventions. He was self-sufficient and enjoyed working with his hands, but if a task was beyond his capability he had no problem enlisting others' expertise, though he gave extensive instructions to any craftsmen with whom he worked.

Franklin's search for a glass armonica builder eventually led him to Hughes and Company, located at the Cockpit Glasshouse, and the services of Charles James. The instrument was apparently finished in late 1761, as an announcement in the January 12, 1762, *Bristol Journal* trumpeted the new invention: "The celebrated glassy-chord, invented by Mr. Franklin of Philadelphia: who has greatly improved the musical glasses, and formed them into a compleat instrument to accompany the voice; capable of a thorough bass, and never out of tune."

It is not entirely clear why Franklin, not long after, changed the name of his instrument from the "glassy-chord" to the "armonica." He announced the change in his letter to Beccaria, declaring that, "In honour of your musical language, I have borrowed from it the name of this instrument, calling it the Armonica," after the Italian word for harmony, *armonia*. One scholar hypothesizes that Franklin's inherent practicality may have spurred the change. At the time Italy was the Western world's "musical Mecca," the land "to which the western world still turned for diversion and instruction." Franklin, then, may have been trying to ensure its positive response in that crucial country. He felt strongly that the armonica was a valuable addition to the world of music—he thought, in fact, that it might eventually

Benjamin Franklin playing his glass armonica.

achieve more prominence than the piano and the harpsichord. A little flattery toward his famous Italian friend, and Italy, may have been a calculated effort to speed his instrument's acceptance by musicians in the region. "It is an instrument that seems peculiarly adapted to Italian music, especially that of the soft and plaintive kind," Franklin assured Beccaria. Nearly from the start, however, non-Italian individuals added an "H" to the new name, leading to the misconception that Franklin invented the mouth organ.

An ad by Charles James in *Jackson's Oxford Journal* in May 1762 gave England notice of the glassy-chord's new name:

The Armonica. Being the musical glasses without water . . . made by Charles James, of Purpool Lane, near Gray's Inn, London. N.B.—The maker is the person who has been employed in the management of the Glass Machines from the beginning, by the ingenious and well-known inventor.

The curious lack of mention of Franklin's name in the notice may have been because Franklin was unhappy with the quality of James's glassblowing. When he ordered another instrument from the Cockpit Glasshouse, he specifically asked for a different workman. That didn't stop James from self-promoting, however. When he opened his own business that June, James advertised himself in the *London Journal* as "the maker who has been employed by the gentleman who is the real inventor, in the first ever made in England, and continues to be honored with his approbation." A few weeks later, James wrote that the armonica "may be so constructed, as to be either a Portable Instrument, or Genteel Piece of Furniture."

Franklin was annoyed by the situation, but he was two months away from returning to Philadelphia, and his days were filled with more important matters. Still, a letter he wrote the following year to Polly Stevenson shows his frustration with the services of the Cockpit Glasshouse in general:

> I am vex'd with Mr. James that he has been so dilatory in Mr. Maddison's armonica. I was unlucky in both the workmen that I permitted to undertake making those instruments. The first was fanciful, and could never work to the purpose, because he was ever conceiving some new Improvement that answer'd no end: the other is absolutely idle. I have recommended a number to him from hence, but must stop my hand.

Whatever the quality of the workmanship, the instruments cost about 40 guineas to manufacture. Over time, however, more makers joined the field, apparently driving down the price. When, years later, in 1787, Thomas Jefferson asked a friend in London about "the price of a good harmonica, the glasses fixed on an axis, to comprehend 6 octaves . . . in a plain mahogany case," he was told that a company named Longman and Broderip would build a three-octave instrument for 30 guineas.

Franklin led a vigorous social life in England, and later on the Continent, and his newly built armonica became a constant at the parties he attended. A skilled player of his musical invention, he spent so many hours entertaining others with the instrument that Thomas Penn complained in a 1761 letter to Pennsylvania's governor that Franklin seemed to be wasting all his time on philosophical matters and "musical performances on glasses." Franklin's audiences, however, were charmed by his performances. Lines from a contemporary novel, Oliver Goldsmith's *The Vicar of Wakefield*, indicate the instrument's rapidly expanding popularity among the English elite: "The two ladies . . . would talk of nothing but high life, and high lived company, with other fashionable topics, such as pictures, taste, Shakespeare and the musical glasses."

When Franklin returned in late 1762 he brought his armonica with him. A December 3 letter from Ann Graeme, the mother of a young woman whom Franklin's son William had recently broken up with, mentions an uncomfortable visit with the Franklins where the strain was eased when he played "a tune on the Armonica." An old Irish musical dictionary tells how Franklin, soon after his return, crept into his attic and set up the armonica while his wife slept downstairs. She had not yet heard the instrument. As Franklin began to play, drawing forth the armonica's "angelick strains," his wife "awakened with the conviction that she had died and gone to heaven and was listening to the music of the angels."

In the music room, or "blue room," of Franklin's Philadelphia house, his new invention took pride of place. Already Franklin considered the third floor room to be the jewel of his residence, decorating it with "gilt carvings, an ornamental fireplace, and decorative chairs and screens." Now the glass armonica joined his daughter Sally's prized harpsichord, along with a bell harp, a Welsh harp, a viola da gamba, and tuned bells. Franklin loved playing duets with Sally, she on the harpsichord and he on his invention. As Franklin wrote to Beccaria, "I play some of the softest Tunes on my Armonica, with which Entertainment our

People here are quite charmed." He seems to have taken an armonica with him to every place he lived for the rest of his life.

Franklin felt so strongly about his invention that he even believed it had the power to heal—as did others, apparently. When Princess Izabella Czartoryska of Poland first met Franklin, she was bedridden, suffering from illness and deep depression, and she was in the process of writing her will and farewell letters. According to the princess, Franklin gazed down at her with his "noble face" in "an expression of engaging kindness." "Poor young lady," he murmured, as he took her hands. He then opened up his armonica, sat down, and began to play. The music made such a strong impression on Princess Izabella that tears flowed from her eyes. Eventually Franklin stopped playing, and came back to the princess's side. Looking at her compassionately, he announced, "Madame, you are cured." And indeed, the princess wrote, "In that moment, I was cured of my melancholia." When Franklin offered to teach her how to play the armonica, she accepted without hesitation, and ultimately sat for twelve lessons with the instrument's creator.

+ + +

To get a sense of how the armonica fit into Franklin's everyday life, let's look at one of the more notable moments of his eighty-four years: the night in 1781 that he received word of the American and French victory over Lord Cornwallis's British troops at Yorktown. This British surrender essentially ended the Revolutionary War.

At the time Franklin was ensconced in his comfortable home in the Paris suburb of Passy, serving as America's first ambassador to France. His guest that November night was twenty-three-year-old Elkanah Watson, future founder of the State Bank of Albany, and a voluminous diarist. Writing in his journal, Watson remarked upon Franklin's urbane manner, his venerable, shoulder-length hair, and his reverence-inducing air of dignity, which was offset by a demeanor so relaxed that Watson felt "perfectly at ease in his presence." Watson knew well that Franklin loved adoration, but the elder statesman's method of wooing it was so subtle that it detracted nothing from his "sterling merit."

After briefly discussing the traitorous American diplomat Silas Deane, Franklin inquired whether Watson knew that he, Franklin, was a musician. Like a proud father, he then led the young man across the room to show off his glass armonica. When Watson requested a performance, Franklin didn't hesitate: he sat down, wet his fingers on a moistened sponge, and launched into one of his beloved Scottish pastoral tunes. The "sweet, delicate" melody thrilled Watson to his "very soul." Beyond that, Watson wrote, the novel scenario proved "highly gratifying to my high toned American pride, to contemplate a native son of my native state, a distinguished philosopher in his 76th year, exhibiting an instrument of his own invention."

The dinner that night was given over to discussion of the fighting in Virginia, and spirited debate of America's revolutionary prospects. As Franklin veered between "gloomy despondency" and exhilarated hope, Watson was struck by how Franklin's "whole machinery" remained in "active play," with no sign of his advancing age. Franklin's mind remained as agile as ever, and he exuded energy.

Watson returned to Paris that night deeply worried about America's potential defeat in the war. He was woken at dawn by a knocking on his door and a message from Franklin. Soon after Watson had departed the previous night, Franklin received a letter from the prime minister of France declaring that "the Combin'd Armies of France & America have forced General

Cornwallis to capitulate. The English Garrison came out . . . & laid down their arms as Prisoners." Needless to say, both Franklin and Watson were ecstatic. Watson's excitement radiated off the page as he wrote that "the American character now rose to an enviable height—the joy of all classes of people was excessive. Paris was brilliantly illuminated three successive nights on this glorious occasion. . . . On my return to Nantes I found all the Cities in my rout in a blaze of illumination."

The historic, once-in-a-lifetime occasion aside, Watson's visit with Franklin illustrates the deep pleasure Franklin took from his glass armonica. Within a few minutes of his young guest's arrival, Franklin had steered him toward his prized invention, and commenced playing the Scottish tunes that were his lifelong delight. We see also that the armonica was more than just a novel musical contraption. It represented American ingenuity and self-respect, the clever, can-do energy the nation needed to harness in order to thrust itself out of the shadow of British rule. In that regard, the armonica resembled nothing so much as its remarkable inventor, Benjamin Franklin, himself.

4

A BRIEF HISTORY
OF GLASS

Franklin's invention of the armonica would not have been possible without the rich history of glass that preceded it. It is impossible to overstate the importance of glass to the development of civilizations past and present; our contemporary world would be unutterably different without it. It is a substance so omnipresent that many of us give it little serious thought. But as scholars Alan Macfarlane and Gerry Martin describe, waking up in a world without glass would be foreign beyond comprehension. There would be no alarm clock or watch to grope for, because both require glass facing. There would be no light to switch on, for there would be no glass bulbs. Draw back the curtains, and air would come pouring through glassless windows. Without clear mirrors, shaving would be an ordeal. At breakfast there would be no glass utensils, bowls, or cups—nor anything made of related substances like plastics, which owe their existence to glass. No television would sit in the living room.

Outside, no cars, buses, or trains would transport you to work, and no airplanes would fly overhead. The shops downtown would have no front display windows. Walking home at night the only streetlights would be torches. Your home's central heating would owe "more to the Romans than the Victorians," and you would tremble from the chill in the meager candlelight. Nor, whether day or night, would there be any spectacles or contact lenses to help you see.

It is not just glass objects that would not exist. There would almost certainly be no running water, either. Nor would we likely have any electricity without the gas and steam engines that first generated it, and that relied on glass for their creation. Say goodbye, then, to computers and radios, to electric stoves and microwaves and refrigerators.

In medicine, the world of viruses and bacteria would remain completely opaque, nor would there be any antibiotics or the profound discoveries in molecular biology that the discovery of DNA allowed for. Our knowledge and understanding of space, meanwhile, would be no more advanced than that of the ancients. We would possess no exact means of measuring latitude and longitude, and if we were lost, we would have no radar, telephone, CB radio, or telegraph to assist us. In the worlds of arts and entertainment, we would have no photographs, no films or television.

Ours, then, is what Macfarlane and Martin call a "glass-soaked" world, one in which glass doesn't just provide, like wood, stone, or clay, shelter and storage. Rather, glass combines any number of practical uses with "the ability to extend the most potent of our senses, sight, and the most formidable of human organs, the brain." Imagine our understanding of science without telescopes, microscopes, thermometers, test tubes, beakers, and glass slides. Glass enables us to capture and store and communicate precise images of nature over any distance. Without glass, there are essentially no elements of our technology-driven civilization that would even exist.

The ancient Roman soldier, statesman, and scholar Pliny the Elder's massive AD 78 opus, *Natural History*, relates the tale of how glass was supposedly discovered. In Pliny's account, a group of traveling merchants moored their boat, which carried a load of potassium nitrate, in a brackish river in the Phoenice region of ancient Syria (today's northern Israel). Disembarking from their ship in order to prepare a meal, the merchants could find no rocks on which to balance their cooking pots, so they used lumps of their potassium nitrate instead. When the fires they lit combined with the potassium nitrate and the sandy seashore, the merchants witnessed "transparent streams flowing forth of a liquid hitherto unknown; this, it is said, was the origin of glass."

The Romans of Pliny's time knew that glass was made largely of sand, and that ancient glassmakers used potassium nitrate to help melt that sand. But the rest of Pliny's story, while evocative, is a fiction. Forms of glass, especially obsidian, exist in nature, primarily as the result of volcanic explosions. But the origins of human-made glass, though thousands of years old, remain murky. Archaeologists posit that glassmaking began in ancient Mesopotamia (contemporary Iraq and Syria) more than four thousand years ago, but only a small number of formless chunks remain as Bronze Age relics. It is only around 1550 BC that the picture grows clearer. During this period, glass vessels in northern Mesopotamia were produced by core forming, a technique in which molten glass is molded around a core of clay and dung with a metal rod at the center. Bright colors and patterns marked the design of these vessels, with

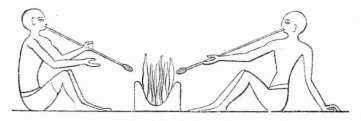

Phoenician glass shop.

the colors coming from various oxides that were mixed in with the raw materials.

More evidence from this period comes from Egypt, where the dry climate and the ancient practice of burying such valuable objects as beads, pendants, and amulets with the dead ultimately resulted in the modern-day recovery of numerous datable items. When Thutmosis II led a victorious war effort in Syria during the second millennium BC, he may have brought back to Egypt captured glassmakers, and the techniques they had innovated, as the spoils of victory. The core-formed Egyptian glass objects from this time mirror the shape of familiar stone and pottery-made items, while such decorative colors as dark blue lapis lazuli and off-white alabaster suggest that the region's glassmakers, who likely worked solely in royal workshops, quickly realized glass's jewel-like possibilities. Glass objects were also utilized during this period as containers for valuable cosmetics and medicine. When the New Kingdom collapsed, around 1070 BC, glass apparently disappeared from use. The breakdown of cities and states along the Mediterranean during this period had a disastrous effect on all advanced technologies and luxury items, glass included.

Two centuries later, the making of glass was revived, as

mighty states roared back to life, heralding the return of city life and markets. The Phoenicians used glass to make fine jewelry, and as a luxury item to decorate high-end furniture. These objects were exported throughout the Near and Middle East. Core-formed glass vessels appeared again in abundance along the Mediterranean, as well. Production of refined glassware continued apace down through the Hellenistic period, when Alexander the Great conquered huge swaths of land in the Mediterranean and Asia. In Alexandria, one of his empire's wealthiest, most influential cities, glassmaking reflected the sophistication, prosperity, and artistry of its citizens. It was also in Alexandria and the Mediterranean region that Hellenistic glassworkers created the first cups, bowls, and jars for eating and drinking. These were luxury objects owned by only the wealthiest individuals.

The onset of the Roman Empire, in the first century BC, coincided with a revolution in glassmaking, which was spurred by the discovery that glass could be blown. Somewhere on the Mediterranean's eastern coast, where Israel and Lebanon now sit, glassmakers invented the method of inflating glass. By the end of the century, glassblowing had overtaken core forming as the most common technique for making glass objects. Glassblowing not only speeded up the glassmaking process, it allowed for a much wider array of shapes and sizes. Because of this, affordable glass objects intended for everyday use were finally made available. Though luxury glass items continued to be produced, they no longer constituted the bulk of the market for glass-based products.

In the next centuries, glassmaking techniques continued to expand and be refined, and not even the sacking of Rome in 410 AD or the horror of the Black Death one thousand years later stopped the mass production of all shapes and sizes of glass objects. And yet we know surprisingly little about the glass produced during the Byzantine Empire, which reigned from the fourth century AD until 1453, when the empire fell to the Ottoman Turks. Glasses, dishes, bowls, cups, and jars were all in common use during this period, and several million tesserae, cube-shaped tiles used in creating mosaics, were manufactured for church-decorating purposes throughout the region.

A more remarkable use of glass developed in Europe during the twelfth and thirteenth centuries, when works of ancient Greek and medieval Muslim scientists were translated into Latin. With this new knowledge, scientists and physicians could use the latest innovations in glassmaking to benefit their research and practice. For example, medieval scientific experiments relied heavily on transparent glass devices, like the still, that would not ruin their contents by rusting or flaking. Doctors at the time used glass devices to prepare the materials they used to treat patients; the see-through quality of glass was particularly useful for observing urine to identify illnesses. Most significantly, Roger Bacon noted in 1268 that "if the letters of a book are viewed through a segment of a sphere [i.e., a lens] . . . they will appear far better and larger." Soon afterward the first spectacles were invented, in Italy.

In the early Islamic period, glassmaking reached its highest point between the tenth and fourteenth centuries. Both everyday, practical items and finely crafted luxury items dotted the landscape, while the practice of blowing glass into molds allowed for objects featuring patterns and intricate ornaments to be produced at almost the same rate as plain items. The Mongol capture of Baghdad in 1258, and the invasions of Iran and India by Timur in the following century, devastated glassmaking capabilities throughout the region, with the result that, from that point on, the elite turned to Europe for their glass-based needs.

Perhaps surprisingly, glassmaking in the Far East seems to have been rather minimal until the formation of the Qing dynasty in the seventeenth century. Before this, Chinese practices appear to have placed much greater emphasis on jade, ceramics, and lacquer than glass. Although Chinese bronze workers had mastered the use of high-temperature furnaces twelve centuries earlier, this technology was not transferred to the production of glass until later. Though beads, garments, pots, and other small objects were produced during earlier dynasties, the establishment by Emperor Kangxi of an imperial glass workshop in Beijing in 1689 first set China on the course of the mass manufacturing of glass. This same period saw the rise of large-scale glass production in Japan, as well. In Korea this level of manufacturing did not occur until centuries later.

In late medieval and Renaissance Europe, meanwhile, Venetian glassmakers developed a reputation as the finest craftsmen in the world. As early as 1224, glassmakers in Venice had formed their own guild, and they specialized in making the thin-walled, often colorless glass called *cristallo*. During Roman and Byzantine times, most glasses produced were too thick to be musical. But the development of *cristallo* set into motion a long trend of producing thin, high-priced glasses for the European elite, which led, indirectly, to the glass armonica's invention. Part of the reason the Venetian glass industry enjoyed such prominence is that it utilized exceptionally pure raw materials: quartz pebbles from northern Italy, soda and plant ash from Egypt and Syria. The government, too, played a continuing role in attempting to control and ensure Venetian glass's excellence. In the fifteenth century, glass expert David Whitehouse tells us, the range of Venetian glassmakers suddenly "exploded like a magnificent display of fireworks," with a variety of richly colored glasses and intricately gilded and enameled glassware pouring forth from the region's furnaces.

Throughout Renaissance Europe, Venetian glass functioned as a status symbol, a dramatic sign of the owner's affluence and fine taste. The glass's clarity, its complex forms and vividness, its delicacy—all of these played to consumers' preferences and interests. Foreign rulers and commercial dealers plied Venetian glassmakers with lucrative offers of employment, but the Venetian government passed strict laws banning glassmakers from migrating to other countries. Some master craftsmen took their chances and fled anyway, but many more plied their trade instead as artistic consultants, assisting in the establishment of local workshops throughout Europe. Foreign glass made "in the manner of Venice" was frequently indistinguishable from the original thing. Much of the glass produced in Austria, France, Belgium, and elsewhere benefited from royal patronage, though common taverns also seem to have used wineglasses to serve their wares.

In seventeenth-century England, parliamentary concerns that glassworks and iron foundries were devastating the country's forests put a damper on the production of glass. The government's concern was not environmental. Rather, it was worried that deforestation would negatively impact the British navy's shipbuilding capabilities. At the same time, the English Civil War from 1642 to 1651 ruined the market for luxury goods, further damaging the country's glassmaking industry. But the monarchy's reinstatement a decade later, and the rebuilding of London following that decade's Great Fire, put the industry back on track. In the century that followed, English glassmakers took the lead in crafting superior vessels, both plain and elegant, for imbibing alcohol and other liquids.

By the nineteenth century, a serious fissure began to appear throughout Europe between those who embraced the increasing mechanization of the glass industry, which was enabled by the widespread use of presses and the invention of machines capable of glass etching, and the artists, critics, and designers who railed against the conformity and coldness of mechanical production. This same fissure appeared in America, where the production of glass dated to the establishment of the colony at Jamestown in 1608. A small glassmaking factory there staffed by Germans and Poles lasted for slightly more than a year.

Elsewhere in seventeenth-century America, glass factories were established at Salem, Philadelphia, and New Amsterdam (New York), but like the Jamestown factory, they all failed. Glass factories had been built in the Americas—in Mexico and Argentina—during the previous centuries, but they, too, had been unsuccessful. Early American colonists who had the resources to do so turned instead to England and the Low Countries for their windowpanes and bottles and other stemware. George Washington imported more than one thousand windowpanes between 1757 and 1773 for his plantation at Mount Vernon.

It wasn't until the eighteenth century was well under way that glassmaking finally established a strong foothold in America. A German immigrant named Caspar Wistar, who had moved to Philadelphia more than twenty years earlier, became America's first flourishing glassmaker when he established a factory in southwestern New Jersey in 1738. Here he produced over 15,000 bottles a year, with an equal emphasis on window glass. He also manufactured scientific equipment, including the kind Benjamin Franklin employed in his research on electricity.

The Revolutionary War a few decades later proved so damaging to commerce and trade that the American glass factories were forced to close. But in the 1780s, with the war finally won, the American glass industry sprang back to life. The rapid expansion of settlements beyond the first thirteen states drove the demand for glass into overdrive. Pioneers heading west needed glass and utensils for their new houses and buildings. Pittsburgh, one of the west's primary gateways, became the hub of this frenetic glassmaking activity, though glassworks also appeared in numerous other states. Into the next century, windowpanes and bottles remained the primary products produced by the country's bustling glass factories, even as fine tableware and lighting devices began making an appearance, too.

In the 1820s, a new technique known as "pressing" enabled a leap in mass-producing glass. Decades earlier, glassmakers in Europe had begun employing handheld presses to fashion such small items as prisms for chandeliers. When combined with molds, the new American presses, embraced by such modernizers as Benjamin Bakewell, not only brought down costs, they increased productivity to such a degree that, in David Whitehouse's words, they represented "the most effective innovation in glassmaking since the discovery of glass-blowing." While becoming a master glassblower required years of training and practice, it took only a few weeks for a worker to learn how to operate a press. What's more, two press operators working in tandem could produce four times the number of glasses as a team of glassblowers that was two times larger.

While the Civil War disrupted America's glass industry, the postwar Gilded Age, and the attendant fortunes generated through oil, steel, and railroad wealth, drove the market for luxury goods to new heights. This period also sparked a new interest among well-off consumers in so-called art glass, the bright, intricate, decorative glassware that remains popular today. At the end of the nineteenth century, the idea of utilizing glass as an artistic medium in and of itself also took root among such leading designers as Émile Gallé, Louis Tiffany, and, later on, Frederick Carder. The influence of these and other artisans on the world of glass only increased throughout the twentieth century, eventually spawning, in the 1960s, the Studio Glass Movement, which emphasized the artist as designer and creator of unique objects. The movement spread internationally during the 1970s, with more and more artists working in studios of their own, rather than in factories dedicated to mass production.

The last six decades have seen rapid developments not only

A painting of nineteenth-century glassblowing
by Charles Frederic Ulrich.

in how glass is made and used, but also in its constituent components. The speed of this growth would have been unthinkable in earlier times, when two-thousand-year stretches separated major glassmaking advancements. But as Whitehouse points out, in recent years we have seen, among many examples, optical fiber causing "a revolution in communications," defect-free glass being developed for LCDs, and ultra-low-expansion silica glass being used in everything from telescopes to machine tool reference blocks. Change will likely come even more swiftly now that scientists are employing nanotechnology—the manipulation of matter on an atomic, molecular, and supramolecular scale—in their search to perfect glass, and also to invent entirely new types of glass.

5

AN INSTRUMENT SO
GRAND AND HAUNTED:
THE HEYDAY OF THE
GLASS ARMONICA

The glass armonica arrived at a time when the entire spectrum of musical instruments, and the sounds they produced, was being improved and enlarged. Keyboard instruments like the harpsichord, the piano (known as the fortepiano), and the clavichord were developing larger followings the more refined they became. Within this larger context of innovation, the glass armonica proved an ideal fit.

The armonica's invention and heyday occurred during a period in which rationality, analysis, and individualism were displacing traditional ways of thinking. And yet, the familiar term Age of Reason is somewhat of a misnomer, suggesting that the Enlightenment was exclusively about reason, and not emotion or passion. In fact, the urge that drove Mozart and Beethoven and their creative contemporaries to investigate, subvert, and overturn the customs and conventions of the musical styles (and associated forms of artifice) that reigned before them sprang as much from an emphasis on "free intellect" and "sympathy," a form of community in feeling, as from dispassionate analysis. The notion of sympathy rested on the idea that by engaging in unblinkered introspection, one could find common elements that united all people. The job of the enlightened artist, then, as Wye J. Allanbrook put it, was "to move an audience through representation of its own humanity." By so doing, an artist fed an audience's sense of personal and communal virtue.

Perhaps the greatest expression of the Enlightenment's focus on freedom and individual empowerment via the accumulation of knowledge was the *Encylopédie*, a massive, thirty-five-volume attempt to compile and disseminate every known piece of scientific knowledge. Edited by Denis Diderot and Jean d'Alembert, the hugely influential *Encyclopédie* was hailed by the intelligentsia, but condemned by the Jesuits. State censorship only enhanced the project's reputation as a contemporary (and deliciously forbidden) Tree of Knowledge. As it happens, that tree included, among its many branches, an entry on the musical glasses. "For many years one has imagined producing, with the help of glasses, a new type of harmony, very pleasing to the ear," the entry reads.

> The instrument which is useful for this effect is an oblong ... box, in which are arranged & fixed several round glasses of different diameters, in which one puts water of various quantities. While rubbing with the wet finger on the edges of these glasses ... one draws from them some very-soft, very melodious & very-constant sounds; & one can play extremely pleasant airs in this manner.

The *Encyclopédie* represented the vogue for learning that had taken root within Europe's growing middle class. This vogue, combined with an expanding audience for the arts, led writers, artists, philosophers, and scientists to shape their works as much (or more) for broad public consumption as for elite authorities and specialists. Novels and plays now portrayed regular citizens, not royals, dealing with commonplace sentiments and concerns. Myriad tracts were written to bring culture to "the people." A sweepingly popular "back to nature" movement, which emphasized emotion in arts and literature, provided a theoretical framework for this democratization of creative and scientific work.

The period also shaded into what science writer Richard Holmes calls the "Age of Wonder," a "second scientific revolution" (in Coleridge's phrase) that, Holmes argues, brought to scientific work "a new imaginative intensity and excitement," centered on a wild, almost uncontrollable "personal commitment to discovery." From here we get the Romantic ideal of the lone scientific genius, à la Mary Shelley's *Frankenstein*, laboring away in pursuit of their *Eureka!* moment, as with the (doubtless apocryphal) story of Isaac Newton being hit on the head by an apple. Particularly in Germany, Holmes writes, this wondrous age favored "a softer 'dynamic' science of invisible powers and mysterious energies, of growth and organic change," a key reason why "the study of electricity," which Benjamin Franklin revolutionized, became the era's "signature science." This was science bound inextricably to passion, a study whose effects could be felt as much in the heart as in the mind.

During this transformational period the audience for live music greatly expanded. As royal patronage diminished, public concerts appeared with increasing frequency in the musical capitals of London, Paris, Vienna, Dublin, and Berlin, vying for attendees with more traditional private concerts and concert societies. The music publishing market, meanwhile, targeted its wares to amateurs, who desired music simple enough for them to master. They also wanted forums where they could read about, and talk about, music. The periodicals of the day regularly featured music, too, and after 1750 music magazines became popular sellers, as well.

Stylistically, the musical period between about 1750 and 1820 is known as the Classical period (this is not to be confused with the tendency today to refer to almost all of the music composed between the sixteenth and nineteenth centuries as "classical"). Haydn, Mozart, Beethoven, and Gluck are the representative geniuses of the period. The decades in which these artists flourished represent a bridge between the Baroque and the Romantic periods. Of course, it is only in retrospect that the term "classical" has been applied. The composers and artists themselves did not think of their work as classical, nor did they for the most part consider their music to be "classic"—they wrote their work quickly, for a contemporary, rapidly shifting market, and they assumed that it would rapidly become outdated. Notable exceptions include Haydn's oratorios and Beethoven's later works, which were consciously written for the ages.

The term "classical" derives, rather, from a comparison to Greek and Roman art, and denotes, at its finest, a high-minded simplicity and balance, an aesthetic stripped of grandiose flour-ishes and overweening ornamentation. It suggests humanism as opposed to romanticism. While Baroque music featured mul-tiple layered lines of independent melody, the mid-eighteenth century saw a shift in preference to the relative clarity of a single melodic voice played over chordal accompaniment. And though the musical forms of the period seem from a modern perspective to have been etched into stone, they were fresh and malleable for the composers who created and deployed them, and were part of an ongoing process of joyous discovery.

According to glass armonica expert Dennis James, eigh-teenth-century music features constant and profound internal subtleties that are "wildly exposed" when you play the armon-ica, as you locate "the ins and outs, the phrasings." The period's music, he says, is

> highly refined, loaded with doctrinal effects, the tiniest re-straints and hesitations. It's almost like seduction—like at court, how you held your fan was communicating huge amounts of subtle sexual information. It's the same thing with eighteenth-century music—it has so much expressive delicacy. Very few instruments reflect that to the degree that

the armonica does. With the period's music, there's constant depth of inflection, and that's one of its greatest joys.

Perhaps most crucially, the late eighteenth century saw the grand ascendance of secular music over sacred music, a remarkable first for the Christian era. As Julian Rushton writes, "The masses and oratorios of Haydn and Beethoven are pinnacles of musical form, not contributions to liturgy." A great canon of secular symphonies, comic opera, choral works, and other forms was explicitly intended to be performed in concert halls, not in churches. The values these works espoused were those of a shared humanity, not those of a rigidly hierarchical Church.

After the glass armonica appeared, it received its first widespread notice via the musical talents of Marianne Davies and her sister Cecilia. Marianne was a youth prodigy, a highly skilled harpsichordist, flautist, and singer. In 1751, at the age of seven, she made her first public appearance, at Hickford's Rooms in London, where she performed a concerto by Handel. In 1753, she put on a similar show, this time in Soho, which her father promoted with an advertisement declaring, "Ye Sacred Muses now attend. A New Song. The Words by a Gentleman on hearing a little Miss perform on the Harpsichord and German Flute and Musick can charm the human heart." Davies carried on in this role throughout the 1750s, playing concerts around London, by herself and with accompanists. The daughter of musician parents—her father was a flautist and composer—she seemed destined for a lifetime of treading the traditional musical path onto which she had been set.

Everything changed, however, in 1761, when Davies met Benjamin Franklin, and he presented her with his newly invented instrument—a remarkable gift, given the glass armonica's high cost. (There is no record of how Franklin and Davies met.) She immediately set to work on mastering it, quickly becoming the armonica's first authentic virtuoso. In February 1762, Davies gave the instrument its world premiere, playing it at the Great Room in Spring Gardens; she followed this with concerts in Bristol and Bath, and, later, Dublin. From this point on, Davies focused solely on the armonica—presumably, in part, because it enabled her to stand out from the crowd of more "common" musicians. A German writer who attended a 1766 performance in Paris reported that Davies, "whom the inventor has endowed with [an armonica], is at present the only person to play it with proper perfection; Mr. Franklin himself is only musical enough to play it for his own enjoyment." The writer had spent the past summer at the Hôtel d'Angleterre in Paris, where he heard Davies perform on the instrument twice daily, and where he had also befriended Franklin.

By 1767, Marianne's younger sister Cecilia, by all accounts a remarkable singer, had joined her on the public stage, performing airs from popular operas. (Cecilia ultimately grew far more famous than her sister.) By this point, the Davies family as a whole had spent years as traveling musicians, playing and singing for audiences in England, France, and Ireland. According to Franklin's friend Mary Rich, Marianne's armonica playing had been heartily embraced by the music-going public.

With an eye toward increasing their exposure to potential patrons, the Davies family set out in 1767 to conquer the Continent more broadly. To do so, they needed letters of introduction from noteworthy friends in London, letters that would testify not only to their family's musical talents, but to their upstanding qualities as human beings. Samuel Johnson, the legendary literary figure, is one of the acquaintances who sang the family's praises, and it was through one of Johnson's friends, the critic and writer Joseph Baretti, that notice of the Davieses spread throughout Italy.

At least seven letters were written by a figure whose very

name is associated with musical genius: Johann Christian Bach, also known as the "English Bach," the youngest son of legendary composer Johann Sebastian Bach. A longtime resident of London, J. C. Bach was himself a composer of significance, and a noted influence on the concerto style of Mozart, an early pupil and lifelong mentee. Bach wrote letters in support of the Davies sisters to potential benefactors in Italy, and to his brothers Karl and Wilhelm, both prestigious composers, in Germany. In his letter to Karl, Bach writes that Marianne "has with her a newly invented instrument, which she plays very well, and which is made of glasses and is played like a clavier." This instrument, he continues, "has such a beautiful effect and brilliance that I am sure that you and everyone else will enjoy it." In addition to praising the sisters' musicianship, Bach takes care, in all of his letters, to emphasize the sisters' "worthy" and "good" characters, as well as their Catholic faith. (He had most likely met the sisters at church.) And indeed, the sisters ultimately received much assistance from their fellow Catholics.

Letters in hand, the Davies family made their way to Germany in fall 1768. They traveled through Mainz, Frankfurt, Mannheim, Schwetzingen, Stuttgart, and Augsburg, collecting additional letters, before arriving at their final destination:

Vienna. There they met the famous composer Christoph Gluck—who, as it happened, had performed in London on the musical glasses in the 1740s—at the Hapsburg court. Through Gluck the sisters received a plum appointment: the Empress Maria Theresa employed them as music teachers for her young daughters. Cecilia gave the girls singing lessons, while Marianne taught them how to play the glass armonica, along other instruments. Two of these girls later became queens of Naples and Spain. The third was Marie Antoinette, the future queen of France.

In Vienna, the Davies sisters also gave regular performances at the Imperial Court, where they soon became high-society favorites. They mingled with the city's finest musicians, as well, such as the immensely famous German composer Johann Adolph Hasse, with whom the sisters lodged. Hasse provided the vehicle for what may have been the pinnacle of the sisters' careers: their performance on June 27, 1769, at the wedding of the Duke of Parma and the Archduchess of Austria. For the occasion, the court poet Pietro Metastasio had written an ode, which Hasse set to music under the title "L'Armonica"; it was likely the first original piece ever written for Franklin's instrument. Marianne played while Cecilia sang accompaniment. Apparently the performance was a great success, for three years later, Metastasio reminisced in a letter about the armonica's beautiful tone, and the skill with which Cecilia pitched her voice so that it matched the instrument exactly.

The Davies family stayed in Vienna until October 1770, when they set out for Italy, with new letters of introduction to Church officials and members of the court in Rome, Naples, Venice, and Milan. When the family arrived in Milan in September 1771, they happened to ride past the lodgings of the Mozarts, where Leopold, the father, and his brilliant offspring, Wolfgang, were standing on the balcony as the Davieses' coach rumbled by. Though there are no records of their previous meetings, the Mozarts and Marianne were apparently well acquainted. Surprised and pleased to see each other, Leopold and Marianne exchanged a quick greeting. A few hours later Leopold set off for the nearby Three Kings inn, the area's most reputable venue, where he assumed the Davies family was staying. Sure enough, he encountered Marianne, Cecilia, and their parents, who could "hardly express their joy" at the unexpected reunion. Johann Hasse's daughter soon joined the scene; she also "was beside herself with delight," having befriended the Davieses in Vienna. In recounting the episode for his wife, the senior Mozart took care to ask, "You will surely remember Miss Davies with her armonica?"

Throughout 1771 and the following year, the sisters' stars continued to rise. Cecilia played a leading role in one of Hasse's operas in Naples, and the family also performed in Rome. In July 1772, an Italian admirer sent a letter to Sir Horace Mann, the British diplomat in Florence, declaring, "I have the honor of presenting to you the sisters Marianne and Cecilia Davies, your compatriots, both musical virtuosi, of whom one sings marvelously, the other plays the harmonica, an entirely new instrument, which corresponds well to its name, and which is unique to this young lady." They continued to attract Italian admirers, such as the talented soprano Tommaso Guarducci, until the following year, when the family finally returned to their London home. Tragedy struck only a month later, in December 1773, when Mr. Davies passed away.

There is little record of the sisters' doings over the next several years, though we know that Cecilia appeared in performances by Sacchini, Traetta, Rauzzini, and Bach. Marianne, however, suffered from health problems, and these increasingly affected the family's musical career. We see this in a letter that Cecilia wrote to Benjamin Franklin in January 1778, when both parties were in Paris:

I hope you will excuse the liberty I take in troubling you with this line but being come to Paris with my Mother and Sister on account of the latter's health, should think myself guilty of an unpardonable neglect were I not to take an opportunity of waiting on the ingenious Inventor of the Divine Armonica. My Sister continues to express her Infinite Obligations to you Sir.

Only five years later, the situation had reached a crisis point. Marianne and Cecilia were in Italy, mourning the death of their mother, who had succumbed after a long and difficult illness. The grief, Marianne wrote, was "almost too much for us to bear." It had set off in Marianne a "violent return" of her "nervous complaints," leaving her near death and confined to her bed for almost a year. This forced Cecilia, consumed with caring for her sister, to turn down several lucrative offers to perform in the theater. Adding to the sisters' travails, the "great and good" Empress Maria Teresa, who would have gladly taken the sisters in, had recently died, as well.

With few options left, Marianne reached out to the man whose invention had changed the trajectory of her career. On April 26, 1783, she wrote Franklin a remarkably open and painful letter requesting his assistance. "Notwithstanding I am at present a being almost insensible to any joy or pleasure this miserable life can afford," she began, "yet as I do still exist, so do in me the strongest feelings of gratitude, respect, and esteem, by which I must always be most sincerely attach'd to my ever dear and worthy friend and benefactor Doctor Franklin." Marianne detailed for Franklin the sisters' "losses and vexation"—so many of them, she confided, that she found herself "heartily disgusted of the world." But all was not lost. Exhibiting a determination born from a lifetime spent as a traveling musician, with all the hardships and deprivations that path entailed, Marianne had plans to resuscitate her musical career. She was practicing again on her armonica, and felt sure that if she could only resume her touring life, traveling among the capital cities, her and Cecilia's fortunes would be reversed. She dreaded the prospect of bringing the instrument on the road again, however, because she remembered the constant fear that the instrument's fragility engendered: at customs houses, in performance spaces—indeed, everywhere—she would be terrified that the instrument might break.

When she was younger, her parents' protection made traveling enjoyable despite this worry, but now, with only a younger sister to accompany her, the prospect seemed overwhelming. But she knew she had to do it. She took courage from the fact that she was "the first public performer" on the armonica, and that, as far as she could tell, "no one else ha[d] made much progress on it," though several had attempted to. "Were I but in Paris under your protection!" she wrote plaintively. But the cost of living there was simply too great given her reduced circumstances.

After so baldly laying out her circumstances, Marianne came to the point of her letter: she wanted Franklin to use his influence to convince the music-loving queen of France, Marie Antoinette—Marianne's former pupil—to provide her with an annual pension. The armonica's invention was "superiorly perfect," Marianne flattered Franklin, and therefore worthy of the queen's patronage—especially because the inventor was "universally ador'd by the French nation." If Franklin would grant Marianne his "usual benevolence," she saw no reason why her plea would be denied.

Marianne had a final request for the old inventor. Because she was trying to make her living by playing the armonica, she wanted Franklin to give his word "that no other Person particularly in the musical Profession should have it in their power to boast of having instructions from Doctor Franklin either for making one of these Instruments, or for the method of playing on it."

What Franklin thought of Marianne's request, or if he even received her letter, we have no record. She wrote him several months later to report that she was "so unfortunate as never to have had any answer," and that she could only conclude the mail delivery had somehow gone awry. We can only speculate at the truth of that assumption, as there is no record of Franklin having responded to her second letter, either.

Marianne tried a different tack, placing a notice in the *Tuscan Gazette* that she, the "original player of the instrument of electrical music called the Armonica," was about to depart Florence, and that anyone who wished to hear her perform—for a final time, presumably—should contact her. By using the phrase "electrical music," William Zeitler writes, Marianne was clearly attempting "to capitalize on Franklin's scientific fame" by linking his dazzling electrical findings to his (completely unrelated) musical invention. Despite her claims of imminent departure, Marianne and her sister remained in Florence for the next two years, their finances dire. Eventually the city's English colony, in a show of compassion, held a fundraiser that allowed the sisters to return home to London.

By the late 1790s, Marianne and Cecilia were eking out a

meager existence as music teachers. Marianne's health, already poor, continued to decline over the next several years, until, around 1818, after decades of hardscrabble living, she finally passed away. Wracked by the loss, Cecilia descended into a serious illness, from which she never fully recovered.

The deaths of her sister and parents, and her continual poverty, made Cecilia's final years a misery. "Every December," she wrote to a friend in 1826, "brings to my recollection the great affliction which it pleased the Almighty to send me, and, which all my resolution can never get the better of." Still grieving for her sister five years later, she wrote, "But allass! I must now be satisfied with the Recollection of the pleasure I enjoyed in travelling as of a pleasing dream never more to be realized having for ever lost that Dear Companion my ever to be lamented Sister whose Society alone could make any spot of the Globe a Paradise to me." When Cecilia died, on July 3, 1835, she was mourned only by a servant and an elderly nurse.

The last known mention of Marianne Davies's armonica— her great gift from Franklin—is in the August 1832 edition of *The Harmonicon*, an influential monthly music journal. The instrument, the journal wrote, "is still in good order, in the possession of a lady who was a favorite pupil of Miss Davies."

✦ ✦ ✦

The armonica's other eighteenth-century virtuoso, Marianne Kirchgessner, was born in Bruchsal, Germany, in 1769, the fifth of seven daughters of a cellist father and pianist mother. Though musical talent ran in the family, none of Kirchgessner's siblings achieved her level of fame. She was marked for difference at age four, when a bout of smallpox blinded her in the aftermath of her mother's death. Her doubly devastated father poured all his resources into curing her, but Kirchgessner remained sightless for life. Undaunted, the young Marianne taught herself piano, showing such skill that a local official sent her to conductor Joseph Schmittbauer for training on the armonica. Schmittbauer, the music director of Karlsruhe, ran an armonica-building factory in the city, from which he produced an instrument specially built for his young charge.

Kirchgessner spent the next decade under Schmittbauer's tutelage, her virtuosity apparent from the start. By the time she turned twenty-one, Schmittbauer, her father, and her royal sponsors all felt she was ready to take her armonica on the road. Kirchgessner's talents were such that the men around her believed a concert tour could make them all rich and famous.

Publisher Heinrich Bossler and his wife, Sophie, became Kirch-gessner's managers, though this relationship soon exceeded its business origins and became a deep and abiding friendship that lasted until her death.

So began an almost ten-year odyssey in which Kirchgessner traveled thousands of miles, crisscrossing the Continent, eventually cutting a path from England all the way to Russia. Her first concert was in Heilbronn in February 1791, an occasion so anticipated that attendees came from great distances to hear her perform. From Heilbronn she made her way to Stuttgart, Munich, Salzburg, and beyond, attracting rave notices along the way. A review of her concert in Linz called her the "famous blind virtuosa," and said that her "heavenly playing on this extraordinarily precious instrument [the armonica] delighted everyone with pure harmony to our ears, utterly exceeding all our expectations." Unlike previous armonica performers, who played only slow, melancholy pieces and relied on "individual howling notes" instead of full chords, Kirchgessner played rich, warm compositions, many of them fast, featuring high-wire trills, and tones that waxed and waned. Several instruments backed her, though they had to be played at minimum volume so as not to overwhelm the armonica's gentle sounds.

Kirchgessner's quick success propelled her on to Vienna, where she remained for several months. Mozart—who had first encountered the armonica almost two decades earlier, when he was seventeen—found her playing so inspiring that he immediately wrote two pieces for her, and began work on a third. This was of a piece with his extremely personal approach to composing. As Paul Johnson writes, Mozart "associated each instrument with particular people he knew who were especially good at playing it," and he always wrote with a specific performer in mind. Kirchgessner performed the first Mozart quintet, Adagio and Rondo, on August 13, 1791. A piece for armonica, viola, flute, cello, and oboe, the quintet soon became a standout in her repertoire. In composing it, Mozart had been sparing in his use of the lower range of tones, as the armonica did not descend below G in the alto register, but the piece is nonetheless regarded as one of the composer's "heavenly" works. As Kirchgessner wrote in the *Vienna Journal*, she hoped the "surpassingly beautiful" composition would convince music connoisseurs that the armonica was "the noblest" of all instruments, "exciting not sad and melancholy," one that enticed "glad, gentle, and elevated feelings." Mozart's second piece for her was titled Adagio for Solo Armonica. In advertising the premiere performance of the piece in Vienna,

Kirchgessner declared that Mozart would be accompanying her on the violin. There are no records of whether this accompaniment actually happened, but if it did, it would have been one of Mozart's final public performances before his death. Either way, the composer began writing a third armonica piece for Kirchgessner, but he died that December—ill, exhausted, and depressed at thirty-five—with only thirteen bars of the composition finished.

Kirchgessner's tour continued into the following year, as she moved throughout Germany and Bohemia. In Berlin she gave four command performances for the king, and received a generous gold reward. The years 1793 and 1794 brought more concerts, this time closer to home, including a performance for Beethoven's teacher, Christian Neefe, which, he reported, "uncommonly agitated" him. In March 1794 Marianne traveled to London, where she appeared in a concert series by Haydn—meaning, most likely, that the famous composer wrote a special sonata for her. A review of the show noted the novelty of her instrument, and said that its "dulcet tones" would be "delightful" in a smaller, less crowded room, where it was not overwhelmed by its musical accompaniment. (Unfortunately, the piece she played has been lost to the ages. Because of her blindness, Kirchgessner learned new music by ear, by having somebody else play it for her. This probably means that fewer hard copies of notations were produced.)

Kirchgessner spent 1795 in London, as well. Under the patronage of the Duchess of York, she performed in Soho for four hours per day: from 1 to 3 p.m., and again from 7 to 9 p.m. This schedule earned her a "small fortune," as it came at a time when solo performances were still a rarity.

She didn't return to Germany until the following year, though Kirchgessner rested in her home country only briefly before alighting for Denmark, where, in 1797, she performed for the king in Copenhagen. She then headed east, to a final destination of St. Petersburg, where Emperor Paul I, son of Catherine the Great, reigned.

By 1800, following her journey to Russia and another two years of performing throughout Germany, Kirchgessner's name was celebrated far and wide. She had befriended many of the era's most notable composers, who had written pieces specifically for her armonica: not just Mozart and Haydn, but also Salieri, Naumann, and Reichardt, among several others. After a decade of life traveling, Kirchgessner had settled, at age thirty-one, into a home in the German countryside, which she shared with her manager and his wife, along with a brood of farm animals and agricultural equipment. Her performing life was far from over, but never again would she travel so far or so frequently.

Over the next several years Kirchgessner played close to home in Germany, with occasional stops in places like Prague, where Goethe visited and heard her play the armonica. Her health received a blow in 1806, when Napoleon's soldiers, after routing the Prussian army at Jena, invaded her house and physically assaulted her, an experience from which she never fully recovered. Her popularity hardly diminished, however. One rapturous review of a Stuttgart performance in November 1808 captures the heady feelings her music continued to evoke:

> Ha, a strange sunshine radiates from me!
> Never have I felt such godly
> Bliss flow over me. I hear
> Eden's clarity, a joyous choir,
> Sounds of Hallelujah ring. . . .
> Thanks be to your magic playing,
> Muse of the armonica!

From Stuttgart, Kirchgessner decided to visit her brother, whom she had not seen in years, in the nearby town of Odenheim. The roads, like many in Europe at the time, were perilous, their risk exacerbated by foul weather. Kirchgessner had endured years of difficult travel in her career, but the fact that she had escaped unharmed had done little to calm her nerves. Narrow roads worried her the most. According to her manager, Heinrich Bossler, "Although she was barely able to see her surroundings . . . she always imagined the worst scenario." Kirchgessner survived the trip to see her brother, but the poor conditions and freezing weather had overpowered her. On the way home, she fell seriously ill, likely with pneumonia, and spent the next week in a fever, occasionally raving. With her manager and a priest at her bedside, Kirchgessner passed away on December 9, after uttering clearly, "Beautiful! Very beautiful!" and calling for her brother and dead sister. She didn't know that her brother had died three days earlier, having contracted her illness.

Bossler felt "destroyed" by the death of the client that he had loved and cared for like a daughter. With "indescribable sadness" he announced her passing to the world. For eighteen years, he wrote, he had watched "her art germinate, bloom, and prosper to the highest maturity," even as she remained free from the egotism and moodiness that marked so many artists. A newspaper obituary seconded this virtuous portrait. Despite frigid temperatures, swarms of admirers walked with Kirchgessner's coffin on the day of her funeral, in a procession headed by the city's noblest families and the entire population of the local music college. The number of visiting mourners was so great that the city's hotels had to call the police to keep order.

If Kirchgessner and Marianne Davies represent the armonica's finest virtuosi, the instrument's greatest showman and raconteur was undoubtedly the German composer Karl Leopold Röllig. Born in Hamburg around 1750, Röllig served as musical director of one of the city's theatrical companies in his early professional years, enjoying success while he was still in his twenties with productions of his now lost opera *Clarisse*. But in 1780, his career took a turn, when he encountered the instrument to which he would dedicate the rest of his working life: the glass armonica.

Even before he had likely developed much skill on the instrument, Röllig set off on a concert tour, performing in Hamburg and Berlin in 1781, and in Dresden as a guest of the highly regarded composer and conductor J. G. Naumann, who praised Röllig's own compositions for their "subtle use of diminished and augmented intervals and harmonies and their resolution." A decade later Röllig moved permanently to Vienna, where he secured a post at the court library and gave regular armonica performances.

Röllig concentrated a great deal of effort on improving the armonica, constantly scouring the glassworks of Hungary and Bohemia in his hunt for the finest glasses. Around 1785 he created a new method of marking the armonica's chromatic glasses—its sharps and flats, equivalent to the black keys on a piano—by ringing them with gold rims. Due to fears of the armonica's harmful effect on players' nerves, Röllig also developed a keyboard mechanism for the instrument as a way to avoid directly touching the glasses, though this keyboard greatly dampened the armonica's unique sound. A persistent inventor, Röllig also created the orphica, a portable three-octave piano that Beethoven employed in two works.

Röllig's real fame, however, came from his showmanship and a deliberately cultivated sense of mystery. He placed gleaming silver candlesticks, their flames alight, on his armonica, and he concealed the instrument's flywheel and treadle in an effort to keep their workings secret. He allowed no one, not even his touring assistant, to peer inside his instrument. Indeed, his penchant for secrecy, and the commercial benefits this aura of mystery could incur, proved so great that he even denied the King of Prussia's request to see the instrument's inner workings. He also refused to sell his instrument no matter how high the offered price.

Röllig further enhanced his eccentric image by publishing stories that purported to report on the armonica's supernatural powers and effects. Though his contemporary W. C. Müller, a music critic and historian, dismissed these efforts as charlatanism, Röllig's stories further separated him from other, more traditional armonica players of his day. Like any raconteur, Röllig began his tales by boasting of the armonica's extraordinary nature, claiming not only that it was "the most beautiful and pleasant instrument ever possessed by mankind," but that there had "never been an instrument more important for the future." He then delved into a series of fanciful, dreamlike anecdotes, many of them supposedly taken from his years of touring, in which the armonica exerted a magical effect on lovers, duelers, children, dogs, entire villages—even an unconscious individual lying in an arbor. At the end of his "Amazing

Stories," Röllig cautioned the reader that the armonica "is no instrument to be used for just sheer amusement; it is worth much more." With his commercial future no doubt in mind, Röllig added, "If you are aware of how much it is worth then it will keep this value forever."

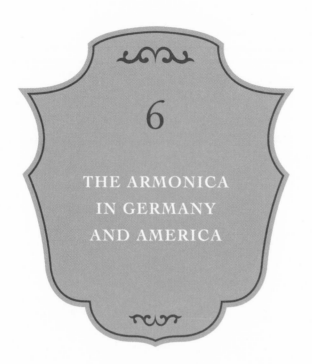

6

THE ARMONICA
IN GERMANY
AND AMERICA

As we have seen, in the late eighteenth century the glass armonica grew fashionable all throughout Europe. Still, no country embraced it with quite the same passion as Röllig's and Marianne Kirchgessner's home base of Germany, where the armonica factory at Karlsruhe produced perhaps the greatest number of instruments. The famous French novelist George Sand mentions this German fervor in her 1856 novel *La Comtesse de Rudolstadt*, during a scene in which her heroine, Consuelo, first encounters the "magical" instrument's "vibrant, penetrating quality." In a remarkable footnote, Sand explains the scene's origins:

> Everyone knows that the armonica created such a sensation with its appearance in Germany, that the imaginations

of poets heard in it supernatural voices, evoked by the celebrants of certain mysteries. For some time this instrument, considered magic before it became popular, was raised by the practitioners of German theosophy to the same divine honor as the lyre among the ancients. . . . From the armonica they evoked one of the hieroglyphic figures in their mysterious iconography, representing in the form of a fantastic dream. Neophytes in secret societies, hearing it for the first time after the terrors and emotions of their harsh initiations, were so deeply affected by it that several fell into ecstasy. They believed they heard the song of the invisible powers.

The hype that Sand describes in her novel shines through in a song composed by the Bohemian musician F. F. Hurka in 1800, based on words by Richter:

Youngest and fairest of the four daughters of sweet harmony, to whom that mother gave omnipotence in magical sounds, thou, sent to comfort mortals whom the goddess saw lamenting, were turned aside from Elysium and did become—"Harmonika." When first every ear hearkened to the new sound, all the sons of earth abandoned themselves to enchantment; their intoxicated spirit seemed to hear the harmony of the spheres and the song of the angels in praise of the uncreated.

These magical effects are also described, Röllig-like, in the writings of Prussian novelist E. T. A. Hoffmann. In an 1819 letter, Hoffmann, in the guise of his music critic alter ego, Kapellmeister Johannes Kreisler, tells the story of his acquaintance, Colonel Tetulow Pripop, a man "totally obsessed" by the armonica. The Colonel spends entire days playing the instrument, wringing from it the "strangest" and most original sounds one can imagine, "distinctive, inimitable" tones that other skilled armonica players only intermittently achieve. The Colonel's manservant, a happy youth with an "endearingly tigerish physiognomy," takes such pleasure in his master's musical stylings that, with loud wails, he throws himself on the ground and kisses the colonel's feet. The manservant is himself a musical virtuoso, a player of idyllic melodies on his Russian pipe, and he recognizes in his master a kindred soul.

Hoffmann writes of the last time he heard the Colonel play his armonica. Emotionally overwhelmed by his playing, the Colonel had removed his enormous fox-fur hat, and the three caps he wore beneath it. Now he sat at the instrument wearing a flowing red cape, drawing forth with his fingers the most "exquisitely ethereal harmonies," while his manservant howled in ecstasy beside him. As if unable to contain such human passion, several of the armonica's glasses abruptly burst into pieces, shattering the scene. Without a word, the Colonel stood up, pulled on a pair of white gloves, and hurried out the door, presumably back to his regiment. And that was that: "I have never seen the good man since," Hoffmann says.

Intriguingly, Hoffmann, in the same letter, critiques the armonica as a "feeble and imperfect" instrument, which, due to its construction, allows only for "slow music played in a strict style," with anything faster sounding "stiff and awkward" and disjointed. He argues that the instrument's tone is responsible for its popularity, not the music that can be drawn from it. This unique tone, he writes, led to a widespread fad in which women swooned at the instrument's sound as a way to attract men. The armonica's popularity "rose during the period of delicate nerves," he says, and popular claims that the instrument "exerted a magical influence on the nerves" led to a corresponding response among well-bred young ladies. For these ladies, it would have been socially unacceptable, when the armonica played, not to

E. T. A. Hoffmann.

"fall into a tolerably convincing swoon," as "she would have risked becoming an immediate object of indifference to any young man of refinement." Even older women were swept up in the fad, fancying themselves "transported back ten or fifteen years by all the pangs of blessed rapture."

Traces of this German rage for the glass armonica can be found even today: Germany's premier music encyclopedia devotes eight pages to the *glasharmonika*, while the equivalent encyclopedia in English allots a mere paragraph. Yet in the eighteenth century the armonica made a splash across the Atlantic, too, among the colonies in America.

The instrument's first recorded American performance was by Stephen Forrage on December 31, 1764, at the Assembly Room in Philadelphia. Benjamin Franklin's newspaper, the *Pennsylvania Gazette*, trumpeted the occasion, declaring the premiere of "the famous Armonica, or Musical Glasses, so much admired for the great sweetness and delicacy of its tone." Four months later, on April 2, 1765, George Washington reported hearing the instrument during a performance in Williamsburg, Virginia. Even before this, Williamsburg's moneyed elite had known of the armonica, with Robert Carter III, the wealthiest colonist of all, paying for one of the new instruments based on the testimony of Bruton Parish Church organist Peter Pelham, who had heard Franklin perform in Philadelphia. (Pelham was eighteenth-century Virginia's most famous musician; he counted Thomas Jefferson among his many fans.)

Robert Carter III was a serious musician, and he apparently became quite proficient on the armonica. In 1773, his children's tutor wrote in his diary of hearing Carter play a song called "Water Parted from the Sea." It was the first time the tutor had heard the instrument, and he found it "charming." "The notes are clear and inexpressibly soft," he wrote, "they swell, and are inexpressibly grand." The armonica was, without question, "the most captivating instrument I have ever heard."

One of America's first poets, the Philadelphian Nathaniel Evans, fell under the armonica's spell, too. After hearing Franklin perform in 1763, he wrote a poem extolling both the instrument and the man, declaring that the armonica "shall join the sacred choir," with its "soft warblings, rolling soft and clear," striking "with celestial ravishment the ear." The instrument's popularity stretched beyond Philadelphia and Williamsburg, with performances recorded over the next several decades in such cities as Boston, New York, Baltimore, and Charleston.

Almost all of the music in America at the time came from

England, as did most of America's professional musicians, joined by their counterparts from Italy and France. As America's economic and political strength increased, so did its musical culture, with new opportunities abounding for music professionals looking for work. It wasn't just new players who found their niche—instrument makers, and producers of printed music, strings, tuning forks, and other associated goods were in demand, too. Along with this shift came the rapid ascension, as in Europe, of secular music over the previously dominant church music. Ballad opera, already a hit in England, swept the country. Towns and cities alike were suddenly alight with public concerts of every stripe, while dancing assemblies proved newly popular, as well. And through it all, from the 1700s until well into the nineteenth century, Benjamin Franklin's hometown of Philadelphia remained the nerve center of this artistic and cultural activity.

7

MESMER AND THE
ARMONICA

$\mathcal{\sim\!\omega\!\sim}$

No individual did more to seed the mythology of the glass armonica and its supposedly unearthly powers than Franz Anton Mesmer, the German physician whose theories of animal magnetism attracted a massive following in Europe and America in the late eighteenth and early nineteenth centuries, and from whose name we derive the word "mesmerized." As Vincent Buranelli writes, by 1789, when the French Revolution broke out, Mesmer was "the most celebrated, notorious, adulated, vilified physician in Europe," hailed variously as a "savior and a charlatan, a genius and a quack."

Mesmer was born in the tree-shaded town of Iznang, in the Lake Constance region of Germany, in 1734. In the distance the majestic Swiss Alps loomed over the lake; not far from the town, the Rhine began its journey to the North Sea. Mesmer's father worked as a groundskeeper for the local prince-bishop, but with nine children to feed, the family's finances were tight. The near poverty of the family's existence heightened the devout Catholicism that permeated Mesmer's home life and his early learning. At age nine, he began his primary education at a monastic school, where he learned the catechism, along with languages and classical literature. But Mesmer's interest lay less in religion than in his favorite subject, music. Both at school and at home, music became his animating passion, one that stayed with him throughout the rest of his long life.

At age sixteen Mesmer entered university in Bavaria, where he studied philosophy. He then moved on to the University of Ingolstadt, where theology ruled the day. By the end of this period of his schooling he was steeped not only in the Jesuit tradition, but in modern philosophical and scientific thought: Copernican astronomy, Cartesian mathematics, Newtonian physics, Kepler's laws of motion. Descartes was a particular favorite, with his insistence that both earthly and heavenly bodies can be interpreted using the same terms, a crucial concept for Mesmer's later theories. Deciding upon graduation that he had no interest in joining the Church, Mesmer enrolled in law school at the University of Vienna, but stayed only a year.

In 1760 Mesmer found the path that suited him: the study of medicine. He spent the next six years in Vienna working on his doctor of medicine degree, while around him Austria battled with Prussia for Central European dominance in the Seven Years War. It was a thrilling time to study medicine in the city. At the time Mesmer attended, the Vienna Medical School, following years of neglect, was flourishing under reforms instituted by the rule of Empress Maria Theresa. In keeping with these reforms, students were taught to focus on bedside observation and a precise rendering of patient symptoms. All over campus, new buildings and clinics were erected, new laboratories established. Because the school's faculty now included many of Europe's brightest medical minds, Mesmer received as fine an education as the Continent had to offer. The latest findings in anatomy, obstetrics, physiology, infectious diseases: all of these were part of Mesmer's learning.

Mesmer's doctoral dissertation bore the eventual title *The Influence of the Planets on the Human Body*, which sounded more resonant of Germany's mystical past than of the Age of Reason. But Mesmer was no occultist. He took a strictly scientific approach to the ways in which the heavenly bodies (that is, gravity) affected human physiology. And indeed, the idea that a patient's symptoms ebbed and flowed with the gravitational impulse of the planets was familiar enough that Mesmer simply copied large sections of his dissertation, including his theoretical framework and all of his case histories, from Richard Mead, the most famous English physician of his day. While plagiarism was somewhat accepted at the time, Mesmer seems to have pushed the practice beyond its usual limits.

At age thirty-two, Mesmer graduated from the Vienna Medical School fully intent on establishing a traditional medical practice. He was an impressive man: well learned in the sciences and humanities, the holder of prestigious degrees, and, by now, an extremely gifted musician on the cello and clavichord, a stylist of passion and finesse. His professors praised his research, and stood ready to accept him into their medical fraternity.

In a move that furthered his reputation, Mesmer married into the Austrian aristocracy soon after he graduated. His wife, Anna Maria von Posch, was wealthy and well connected, and her high social status attached itself to her new husband. Theirs was reportedly the grandest Vienna wedding of 1768. Following their honeymoon, the couple moved into a vast and stylish mansion overlooking the city's main park. Soon Mesmer was hobnobbing with royalty, Austrian and otherwise, as well as with landed magnates and wealthy businessmen. Due to the range of his knowledge, Mesmer was a skilled and popular conversationalist, more than able to hold his own with his newfound friends and relatives.

Suddenly freed from any financial pressures or constraints, Mesmer set up a private medical practice in his home, along with a research laboratory where he engaged in conventional research in chemistry and medicine. To the vast grounds of his estate, layered with gardens and groves, he added an outdoor theater for recitals. He also continued to throw himself into music, spending much of his free time playing the violoncello and clavichord. But his favorite instrument was a recent invention: the glass armonica, which would come to play a crucial role in his medical practices, and which remained Mesmer's instrument of choice throughout his long life. Every week Mesmer held an open house to which the city's highborn music lovers swarmed. He often joined in the performances, playing his armonica on compositions by Purcell, Gluck, Haydn, and his Viennese contemporaries. To flatter their host, the guests usually asked Mesmer to perform solo pieces on his armonica, as well.

Mesmer and his wife were also frequent guests at private concerts in the homes of their wealthy friends. They saw the city's freshest talent, the composers and performers who were currently exciting Vienna's musical elite, and they gossiped with their friends about the musicians' lives and fortunes.

In 1768 the Mesmers heard about the twelve-year-old prodigy who was impressing audiences across Europe: Wolfgang Amadeus Mozart. That year Leopold Mozart brought Wolfgang and his older sister, Maria, to Vienna, to showcase their remarkable talents for the political and cultural elite. The family had first visited the Austrian capital six years earlier, when Wolfgang and his sister had enchanted Empress Maria Theresa and Archduchess Marie Antoinette with their virtuosity. This time, however, the Mozarts received a chillier reception; the palace was still shrouded in gloom from the plague years, and the city's wealthy patrons were far less charmed by a "mature" twelve-year-old Wolfgang than they had been by his younger self. As the Mozarts teetered on the verge of failure, Mesmer came to their rescue. He commissioned from Wolfgang a new composition, the one-act opera *Bastien und Bastienne*. It is not known how the two families met, but Mesmer, with his depth of musical knowledge, had immediately grasped that the young composer was a genius of unrivaled power, not some flash-in-the-pan oddity.

Mozart performed his commissioned work at Mesmer's home in the fall of 1768. Not long after, the Mozarts returned to Salzburg. They did not return to Vienna until 1773, by which point Wolfgang had turned from a preteen prodigy into a brilliant composer, and a refined young man. "Nobody recognized Wolfgang," Leopold Mozart reported to his wife. "You can picture to yourself the joy . . . at seeing us."

Soon after their arrival, the Mozarts paid a visit to the Mesmers, who, Leopold wrote, were "all well and in good form as usual." According to Leopold, once the families had finished lunch, Mesmer played for the Mozarts "on Miss Davie's harmonica or glass instrument and played very well. [The instrument] cost him about fifty ducats and is very beautifully made." One month later, Leopold again mentioned the armonica, telling his wife that Mesmer played it "unusually well," and that young Wolfgang had played upon it, too. "How I should like to have one!" he wrote. Throughout their stay in Vienna, the Mozarts spent many additional hours socializing with the Mesmers, often relaxing in their garden, which Leopold described as "extremely fine, with views and statues, a theater, an aviary, a pigeon-house and, at the top, a belvedere looking right over the Prater."

The Mozarts soon returned to Salzburg, but Wolfgang never forgot his Viennese friend and patron. Years later, in 1790, he included a sly reference to Mesmer in his opera *Così fan tutte*. Mozart, like his father, was a great lover of musical jokes, a Bavarian specialty at the time. Alluding to Mesmer's use of magnets in his medical practice, Mozart wrote,

Here and there a touch
Of the magnet,
The stone of Mesmer
Who was born and bred
In Germany,
And became so famous
In France.

During the 1770s, a young relative of Frau Mesmer's named Francisca Oesterlin came to live with the Mesmers in their Vienna mansion. Oesterlin, by all accounts a friendly, engaging woman, suffered from bouts of periodic "hysteria," during which she would spasm, vomit, faint, hallucinate, and experience temporary blinding and paralysis. These episodes lasted for days at a time, rendering Oesterlin unable to care for herself. Mesmer was concerned with and intrigued by his houseguest's symptoms. As a physician, he engaged her in the conventional treatments prescribed for hysteria, including drugs, electrotherapy, bleeding, and purging. Oesterlin's condition, however, remained unchanged.

Mesmer concluded that orthodox medicine was not the answer, and began to search for solutions elsewhere. As he looked over his clinical notes, he realized that Oesterlin's symptoms followed a recurring pattern of crisis and improvement. He connected this pattern with the extravagant cosmology that he had espoused in his dissertation, *The Influence of the Planets on the Human Body*. Oesterlin, Mesmer determined, was suffering the effects of the "universal fluid"—the planet-controlled "animal gravity" that "ebbs and flows" through our bodies. To cure Oesterlin's symptoms, he needed a way of managing this cycle, in the same way that the moon controls the tides.

Mesmer soon hit upon a solution: magnets. A number of medical professionals at the time promoted the use of magnets in healing, though just as many argued against their effectiveness. For Mesmer, magnets connected logically with his concept of a universal fluid that surges and recedes within us. As he wrote, "The magnetic influence of the heavens affects all parts of the body, and has a direct effect on the nerves. Consequently, an active magnetic force must exist in our bodies."

After procuring a set of magnets from a university colleague, Mesmer put them to use. On July 28, 1774, as Oesterlin suffered another attack, Mesmer placed magnets on her stomach and legs. "Almost immediately," he reported, "she began to show severe symptoms," with "painful volatile currents" shooting through her body. Soon, however, the currents "flowed downward to her extremities," and the symptoms were alleviated. A six-hour period of rest followed. The next day, when Oesterlin's symptoms returned, Mesmer repeated his treatment, with the same results. He felt certain, as Vincent Buranelli writes, that "he was generating artificial tides in her nervous system"—in other words, he was "controlling the ebb and flow of the universal fluid."

Mesmer felt the magnets were simply *conductors* of the universal fluid, not the agents of it, and so he began experimenting on Oesterlin with nonmagnetic objects, like cloth and wood. Again, his results were successful. This led Mesmer to his key insight, or, more accurately, his key delusion: if nonmagnetic objects were effective in channeling animal magnetism, it was because Mesmer himself was handling them. He, then, was the animal magnet—he had the particular ability to "magnetize" the objects. As such, his powers were comparable to the effect of a mineral magnet on metal. In Mesmer's mind, he had hit upon an earth-shaking discovery.

Mesmer claimed further that there existed only a single disease, which expressed itself through a wide array of symptoms. This one disease resulted from "obstruction of the flow of animal magnetism inside the human body." To cure the disease, one needed to apply animal magnetism, thereby restoring the body's natural balance and flow. Again, Mesmer believed this to be a landmark discovery in the history of human medicine.

Imagine his dismay, then, when his medical colleagues in Vienna proved highly skeptical of his claims. They believed in traditional physiological medicine; animal magnetism reeked of occultism. If anything, Mesmer's experiences with Oesterlin indicated that he had mastered the power of suggestion, not cosmological healing. He had, in effect, hypnotized the patient.

When Mesmer revealed his experiments with Oesterlin to Jan Ingenhousz, the Dutch physician who discovered photosynthesis, Ingenhousz denounced him. Mesmer was stunned. Ingenhousz was an influential member of the Royal Society, recruited by none other than Benjamin Franklin. He now became a relentless critic of Mesmer. In 1778, when Franklin was in Paris, Ingenhousz wrote the famous American a letter: "I hear . . . the Vienna conjuror Dr. Mesmer is at Paris, [and] that he still pretends a magnetical effluvium streams from his finger and enters the body of any person without being obstructed by walls or any other obstacles." This "stuff," Ingenhousz continued, was "too insipid" to be believed "by any old woman."

Mesmer responded to his critics by going over their heads: he appealed to the general public directly, and his Vienna office soon swarmed with patients drawn to his "magical" powers. The more dismissive Mesmer's fellow physicians became of his efforts, the more patients packed his waiting room. These patients believed—desperately *needed* to believe—in Mesmer's powers of animal magnetism, and if, in truth, his actions were more those of a faith healer than a physician, the results could nonetheless be impressive. He cured mental and physical afflictions alike, and he soon developed followers throughout Austria and the German states.

The Viennese establishment's criticism of Mesmer continued to grow. It reached a peak in 1777, when Mesmer failed, despite great fanfare, to cure the blindness of eighteen-year-old pianist Maria Theresa Paradis, whose father was the empress's private secretary. A scandal erupted, with the parents accusing Mesmer of performing risky experiments on their daughter, and keeping her in his clinic against their will. Gossip flowed freely: what was Mesmer doing with a blind teenage girl, in private, behind locked doors? (Suspicions about Mesmer's behavior with his female patients would follow him throughout his life.) The Paradis case proved to be a final straw: the empress ordered Mesmer to stop "all this nonsense," and his university colleagues talked of expelling him from the faculty.

If Vienna would not accept Mesmer, then Mesmer would not accept Vienna. In February 1778 he moved to Paris, where he set up shop in a luxurious suite at the Place Vendôme. He was hardly an unknown entity, his ideas having already been promulgated in French intellectual and scientific journals. He arrived at a heady time in the French capital. The ideas of Newton, that god of science, and a key influence on Mesmer, reigned over the city. The works of Voltaire and Rousseau, both of whom died that same year, had attracted legions of followers. Mesmer came to Paris as a scientist seeking to join, however naively, the scientific elite. But from the start, his practices found much greater resonance among the occultists, who felt he was one of them. He

Franz Mesmer.

gained only one follower, the royal physician Charles d'Eslon, among the city's medical establishment.

The lack of "respectable" acceptance hardly affected Mesmer's popularity, however. His clinic proved so successful that he soon had to transfer to larger quarters, in the city of Créteil, outside Paris, where he lived in a house among his patients. Here he began to perfect his group therapy—or, in more accurate terms, his séances, a method of mass treatment that allowed him to treat dozens of patients a day. He stocked his séance room with baquets, large wooden tubs, which he filled with water and lined with "magnetized" bottles, as well as pieces of metal and stone. Mesmer claimed to have magnetized these objects through his powers of animal magnetism. Iron poles jutting out from the tubs served as conductors. His patients, most of whom were wealthy, aristocratic Parisians, rubbed their ailing bodies on the poles, while also holding each other's hands to increase the "current." Mesmer would stride through the room in flowing clothes, checking each patient individually.

Mesmer took great care to foster an atmosphere in his séances that would increase his patients' receptivity to his methods. His emphasis was on creating a rapport by which they would place their total faith in him. This, he thought, increased their receptivity to his animal magnetism. Knowing that imagination and suggestion were key to this process, he designed his séances as if he were producing a play. Heavy drapes covered the windows, creating a faint, warm light. Patients could talk only in whispers, and only to Mesmer and his assistants, not to each other. At times the only sound was the heavy breathing of patients as the séances reached their pitch.

The glass armonica played a crucial role in these séances. Mesmer would play his instrument not only to set the mood, but also because he believed the armonica's music promoted the flow of animal magnetism into his patients. As he stated in his memoir, animal magnetism could be "communicated, propagated, and reinforced by sound." He thought each patient needed to be brought to an emotional peak, almost a breaking point, before their healing could begin. The armonica enhanced this, and fed the group contagion that the séances fostered. Patients would often shake and faint, in the manner of a tent revival meeting. They would be moved to a padded room until they recovered.

One doctor who attended a séance soon after Mesmer's move to Créteil described the scene. He had brought along a friend, an army surgeon, who suffered from gout:

After several turns around the room, Mr. Mesmer unbuttoned the patient's shirt and, moving back somewhat, placed his finger against the part affected. My friend felt a tickling pain. Mr. Mesmer then moved his finger perpendicularly across his abdomen and chest, and the pain followed the finger exactly. He then asked the patient to extend his index finger and pointed his own finger toward it . . . whereupon my friend felt an electric tingling. . . . Mr. Mesmer then seated him near the harmonica; he had hardly begun to play when my friend was affected emotionally, trembled, lost his breath, changed color, and felt pulled to the floor.

In one instance, Mesmer's armonica music even overwhelmed his assistant. According to Frank Pattie, "Mesmer experimented on [d'Eslon] by playing on the glass harmonica . . . and conveying animal magnetism to him. D'Eslon was obliged to beg for mercy about the music, presumably because of the discomfort caused by the charge of animal magnetism which it carried."

Mesmer continued playing the armonica during his nonworking hours, as well. In 1779 he played for the famous composer Christoph Gluck, who was so impressed that he

Image of a typical Franz Mesmer séance.

recommended Mesmer begin improvising his own melodies rather than sticking to sheet music.

Mesmer's séances proved remarkably successful, with scores of patients declaring their nervous disorders and physiological problems cured. Mesmer attempted to use these successes to gain the approval of the Royal Society of Medicine, the Paris Faculty of Medicine, and the French Academy of Sciences. As in Vienna, however, the medical establishment rejected him. They declared his cases inconclusive and nonscientific—some of the cures might have been partial, some might have been faked, some might have been nature working on its own. Mesmer, who believed his evidence to be ironclad, was shocked and infuriated.

In late 1779, desperate for help in establishing animal magnetism as a legitimate practice, Mesmer reached out to one of the world's great thinkers on electricity—and, as it happened, the inventor of Mesmer's beloved glass armonica. He invited Benjamin Franklin, along with Franklin's friend Madame Brillon, to hear him perform on the instrument. In reality, Brillon later wrote, Mesmer was more concerned with discussing "electrical fluid" than with showing off his armonica-playing skills. Franklin himself had, decades earlier, experimented with electricity as a treatment for nervous diseases and paralyses, but he had found the results lacking. He thought "electrical cures," such as they were, might be more a panacea than anything. Unsurprisingly, he found Mesmer's concept of animal magnetism unconvincing at best, and fraudulent at worst.

But Franklin's and Mesmer's lives would continue to intertwine. Inspired by the Freemasons, Mesmer created the Society of Harmony in 1783 to promote his ideas throughout the culture. The Freemasons, like Mesmer, were passionate proponents of glass music, believing that it fostered human harmony. The Society of Harmony was a Mesmerian academy, a combination institute and medical clinic that taught its adherents the practice of animal magnetism. In effect, it was a secret society, one of many that dotted the French landscape at the time. With its dedication to human betterment, the society attracted such disciples as the Marquis de Lafayette, who praised Mesmer in his letters to George Washington. More relevant, it attracted William Temple Franklin, Benjamin Franklin's grandson.

It may have been concern over his grandson's welfare that inspired Franklin to continue investigating Mesmer's techniques. In 1784, five years after his first encounter with Mesmer, Franklin's doubts about animal magnetism remained undiminished. In a letter that year, he wrote:

I cannot but fear that the expectation of great advantage from this new method of treating disease will prove a delusion. . . . There are in every great, rich city, a number of persons who are never in health, because they are fond of medicines. . . . If these people can be persuaded to forbear their drugs, in expectation of being cured by only the physician's finger, or an iron rod pointing at them, they may possibly find good effects, though they mistake the cause.

That same year, Louis XVI established two commissions to investigate Mesmerism. The prodding came from Mesmer's former follower, d'Eslon, who had broken from his increasingly controlling and intransigent mentor, and now wanted to prove the worth of animal magnetism on his own. The king appointed Franklin, then the seventy-eight-year-old American minister to France, to head the first and most important commission. His colleagues included Jean Bailly, France's leading astronomer, Antoine Lavoisier, the founder of modern chemistry, and Joseph Guillotin, namesake of that "humane" instrument of execution.

Franklin's commissioners embarked on a months-long series of experiments to determine the validity of animal magnetism. They did not doubt the reported cures; their interest lay in the *cause* of the cures. First they visited d'Eslon's clinic and examined the tools of the trade—the baquets, the iron rods, the armonica—and witnessed the convulsions, the faintings, the trances, and the supposed healing of d'Eslon's patients. Some of the commission members spent long hours at the baquets, attempting in vain to have themselves magnetized. As David Gallo and Stanley Finger report, they also "told some [patients] that nonmagnetized objects were magnetized . . . and had still others magnetized without them knowing about it." They lied to one patient that d'Eslon was in an adjacent room directing universal fluid at her, whereupon she immediately fell into convulsions.

Due to Franklin's ailing health, some of the commission's experiments took place at his residence in Passy. In one notable instance, d'Eslon claimed to have magnetized an apricot tree in Franklin's yard. D'Eslon then directed one of his patients, a sensitive, infirm young boy, to wander the grounds, on the theory that the boy would enter a crisis state when he neared the tree. The boy did indeed have a crisis—but at the wrong tree. A similar experiment at Lavoisier's residence achieved the same results.

On August 11, 1784, the commission issued its final report,

in which it stated firmly that "nothing proves the existence of the animal magnetic fluid." This "nonexistent fluid," the report continued, was therefore useless—and Mesmerism, by extension, was a sham. What's more, its practice could actually be dangerous, with "all group treatment where the methods of magnetism are employed [ultimately having] harmful effects." With this authoritative damning, the report declared Mesmerism, as a scientific matter, dead.

Franklin heartily supported his commission's findings. One year later, he wrote a letter to Jan Ingenhousz in which he continued to bash the discredited physician:

Mesmer continues . . . and still has some Adherents and some Practice. It is surprising how much Credulity still subsists in the World. I suppose all the Physicians in France put together have not made so much Money during the Time [of Mesmer's residence in Paris] as he has done.

Unsurprisingly, an infuriated Mesmer forcefully rejected the commission's report. He soon abandoned Paris, ultimately returning to the region of his youth to spend his last decades living in comparative obscurity. He had a modest home and a housekeeper to take care of him and keep potential curiosity seekers at bay. He continued to play extensively on his glass armonica, particularly after meals or to honor a valued guest. When he died, he bequeathed the armonica to a close physician friend.

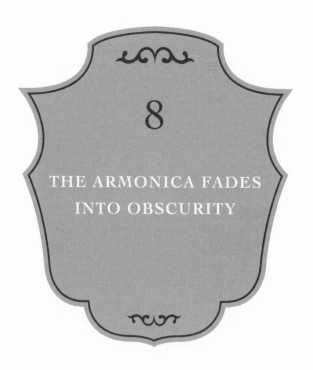

8

THE ARMONICA FADES
INTO OBSCURITY

For all of the glass armonica's popularity during the latter half of the eighteenth century, a darker undercurrent of suspicion, superstition, and fear of the instrument's supposed negative effects on one's physical and mental health existed as well. As the nineteenth century dawned, this alarm grew more prominent, with greater numbers of people connecting the armonica's haunting sounds with illness, insanity, convulsions, fainting, marital disputes, and even death. The instrument's link with Mesmerism, and, by extension, charlatanism, helped to foster these associations. In Germany rumors spread that the instrument could *wake* the dead. After a child died during an armonica performance, fearful politicians and police in some rural areas went so far as to ban the armonica outright.

Writing in 1803, Etienne Sainte-Marie, a member of the Medical Society of Montpelier, fed these concerns, claiming that the "melancholy timbre of the armonica plunges us into a profound detachment, relaxing all the nerves of the body, to the point that a very robust man is not able to listen to it for an hour without becoming ill." Similar claims appeared in the work of the director of the School of Medicine in Toulouse. Opining on the armonica's "strange effects," the director related the story of a young man "prone to melancholy by hereditary effect," who was so in love with playing the armonica that he did so night and day, completely giving himself over to the instrument's "dangerous enjoyment." One day the man's sister received a letter from him stating that the armonica's "extraordinary effects," combined with his depressive nature, had finally pushed him over the edge toward suicide.

This kind of testimony was taken by many as medical gospel. In 1826, Peter Lichtenthal declared that the "nervously infirm should not attempt to play [the armonica] at all." Even healthy people should play the instrument "in moderation," while "those in whom the darker bile resides" should avoid the instrument completely, or, at the very least, play only happy, upbeat melodies on it. Earlier, a Dr. Willich, in his *Lectures on Diet and Regimen,* had declared that, from a dietetical point of view, the armonica deserved to be "condemned," because pressing one's fingers on the glasses was a kind of "negative electricity" that induced "a great degree of nervous weakness." This effect was heightened, Dr. Willich said, by the armonica's "acute and vibrating" tones, which infected the ears.

Controversy over the armonica rose to such a pitch that Friedrich Rochlitz, one of the era's most influential voices on musical matters, felt compelled to step into the fray. Rochlitz had long reigned as the prominent and esteemed editor of the Vienna-based *Allgemeine Musikalische Zeitung* ("General Music Journal"), one of Europe's leading music periodicals, and he hobnobbed easily with such friends as Beethoven and Goethe. As the eighteenth century came to a close, Rochlitz dedicated a lengthy and detailed editorial to getting at the truth regarding the armonica's effect on one's health.

Rochlitz declared that he knew many armonica players, both male and female, all of whom asserted that playing the armonica did no more damage to one's health than any other similar instrument. He then examined the various claims against the armonica, beginning with the notion that the friction of the glass on water-softened skin stimulates the nerves, an action exacerbated by the instrument's vibrations. This he dismissed out of hand, saying that the only negative effect of playing with what today are known as "prune fingers" is that it ruins the instrument's pleasing tones.

Next Rochlitz tackled the belief that the armonica's "piercing and penetrating" sound "violently" shook the body's nervous system, damaging the "nerve roots." This "would be terrible," Rochlitz agreed, "if it were true." However, he said, this claim blamed the instrument itself for the fact that amateur, "unqualified" armonica players had not yet learned how to draw out the instrument's "smoother tone." The players, not the instrument, were to blame. Of course, if a player already suffered from damaged nerves, Rochlitz wrote, the armonica could heighten the effect. But wasn't this true, he asked, of anything that affected the emotions, whether a book, song, or touching scene? Even the "smallest annoyance" or an "interesting conversation" could harm the nerves.

Some detractors, Rochlitz said, blamed the armonica for inducing melancholy, because the instrument was fit primarily for playing slow, mournful tunes. Once this dark mood took hold of a player, the thinking went, further playing caused the depression to become permanent, resulting in "lonely, sad and melancholic

Friedrich Rochlitz.

people." Rochlitz responded by questioning whether it was true that only "sad things" could be played on the instrument, arguing that too many critics had conflated "slow" with "sad." What about all the slow melodies, such as hymns, he asked, that "raise the heart, the courage, leading to a happy prayer, a trustworthy optimism?" In fact, he wrote, it is exactly these sorts of uplifting melodies for which the instrument was best suited, owing to "the swelling of its tones."

All told, Rochlitz declared, he found playing the armonica to be generally harmless. And yet he conceded that there were situations in which players should show care—but this, he said, held true for any activity that plays upon the emotions. So while people with nervous disorders should avoid playing the armonica, they should also avoid any other activity that roused their "disease." Likewise, people who were in a glum mood should steer clear of the armonica—or only play happy tunes—just as they shouldn't read or write or speak anything that intensified their mood. Similarly, people should avoid playing the instrument late at night, because the night's naturally melancholic and isolating atmosphere tended to heighten one's gloom.

Johann Christian Muller, an eighteenth-century German armonica teacher, made many of the same arguments as

Rochlitz in his *Self-Instruction Manual for the Glass Armonica.* "If playing the armonica were to bring the performer gradually closer to death, or at least cause certain illnesses, that would be truly terrible," he wrote. "But where is the evidence?" He cited his many friends and students in Dresden who played the armonica regularly, and suffered no ill effects. Even if the armonica *could* be "enervating," he said, what of the many other enervating agents in life: "harmful novels, false friends, or perhaps a deceiving woman"? If a man or woman suffered from delicate nerves, they should avoid *anything* that might aggravate their condition.

Indeed, of the armonica players we have examined in this book—Benjamin Franklin, Marianne Davies, Marianne Kirchgessner, Franz Mesmer—only Kirchgessner died young, and that was from pneumonia. Franklin and Mesmer both lived into their eighties, while Davies lived to seventy-three—and this at a time when the average lifespan hovered around forty years. By this token, William Zeitler facetiously notes, the armonica could be said to *increase* one's lifespan.

To be understood, then, claims against the armonica must be set within their historical context. In the latter half of the eighteenth century, a new medical and intellectual consensus arose that linked music, in a negative way, to one's nervous system. Medical experts and philosophers alike argued that music's power to overstimulate our fragile, delicate nerves could lead to sickness, loosened morals, and even death.

For most of the Enlightenment, the association between music and stimulation had been framed as an issue of sensibility, not disease. Music was thought to refine the senses, to guide one's moral beacon. It was, in the Pythagorean sense, a representation of the universe's higher order, and, as such, a healthy outlet for the passions. But in the late Enlightenment, as medical professionals came to regard contemporary culture as "sick," a new theory of illness claimed that stimulation was the root cause of all disease. Nervousness, until recently a fashionable sign of refinement, became instead a personal threat. Much as coffee and the novel had in earlier decades, music became fodder for doctors' increasingly critical view of the habits of the elite. The chaos and uncertainty unleashed by the French Revolution, and the newfound suspicion of universal order and kingly rule, tore music from its bond to the mathematical precision of a harmonious heaven—a heaven that was itself viewed with increasing doubt.

Perhaps unsurprisingly, Benjamin Franklin played an

important role in this societal shift. In the early eighteenth century, nerves were connected to medical theories of "animal spirits" and "nervous fluid," similar to Franz Mesmer's theory of animal magnetism. But in the wake of Franklin's discovery that lightning was electricity, and the waves of related research that this discovery unleashed, nerves came to be situated within an electrical framework. From this perspective, music was not a link to universal harmony—instead, like electricity, it had a blunt, immediate impact on your nerves. This physicality represented not only a moral concern, but a serious medical one.

Richard Browne's 1729 book *Medicina Musica* laid the early foundation for this newfound belief in music's effect on the nerves. Browne approached the issue from a Newtonian perspective, viewing it as a given that music's emotional impact was scientifically observable and quantifiable. The sounds that rose from "tremulous Motions of the Air," he claimed, were

> collected by the external Ear, [then] carry'd through the auditory passages to the Drum, on which beating, the four little Bones that are thereby mov'd and they move the internal Air, which, according to Degree of Motion, makes an Impression of the Auditory Nerves in the Labyrinth and Cochlea, so that

according to the various Refractions of the external Air, the internal Air makes various Impressions upon the Auditory Nerve.

For decades this process was thought to be beneficial, with music seen as a healthy means of taming or refining the passions, as in Shakespeare's *Twelfth Night*, when Duke Orsino utters, "If music be the food of love, play on/Give me excess of it, that surfeiting,/The appetite may sicken and so dye." But by the end of the eighteenth century, this view had been turned on its head: music was not a salve for unhinged fervor, but rather its source.

Examples of music's pernicious effect on the nerves were suddenly everywhere. In 1793, English clergyman and author Richard Eastcott argued that the "dangerous" music of composers such as Handel, Arne, and Lampugnani could induce hysterics in listeners. He even claimed that, during a performance of Handel's *Esther* at Westminster Abbey, a chorus singer had died after becoming "violently agitated" by the powerful music. The next year, philosopher Michael Wagner took up Eastcott's argument, writing of a music lover who fell ill and died after playing the triangle. (Yes, the triangle.) Eastcott and Wagner were soon joined by a veritable chorus of music's naysayers, giving rise to a new conception of what James Kennaway calls "pathological music."

This concept, as might be expected, was heavily gendered. Music, in the prevailing viewpoint, preyed on women's "weak" and "delicate" nerves, leading to "sensual," lustful feelings that destroyed a woman's capability to be a "healthy" wife and mother. As Kennaway writes, this social anxiety regarding music's "medical and moral effects on women" found its locus in a single instrument: the glass armonica.

Almost as soon as the armonica was invented, it became associated with female sensuality and physicality. In Heather Hadlock's words, the instrument was "represented as a 'sister' and even as a physical extension of the woman performer," even as the armonica's seemingly disembodied sound also served to "erase" the body of the performer playing it. Other instruments required players to exhibit intensity and nimbleness when performing on them, but the armonica made it appear as if simply laying one's hands on the instrument would produce sound. This, Hadlock says, resolved two seemingly opposing yearnings: "to *hear* women making music" but "to *see* them in a relaxed and graceful attitude." The armonica gave the impression of practically playing itself, offering an immediate leap beyond the clumsy, and therefore unfeminine, initial stages of attempting to learn an instrument. What's more, the lack of virtuoso pieces written for the armonica—unlike those composed for, say, the flute—meant that female players would never make music that was overly demanding, tiring, or noisy, any one of which would have rendered the armonica unsuitable for a "domestic setting."

Because the armonica was viewed as so feminine, it fit within the narrow strictures imposed by the era's notions of female propriety, in which only a few instruments were considered acceptable for women musicians. In *The Young Ladies Conduct*, published in 1772, John Essex argued:

> The *Harpsichord, Spinet, Lute,* and *Base* [sic] *Violin*, are Instruments most agreeable to the Ladies: There are some others that really are unbecoming the Fair Sex; as the *Flute, Violin* and *Hautboy*; the last of which is too Manlike, and would look indecent in a Woman's Mouth; and the *Flute* is very improper, as taking away too much of the Juices, which are otherwise more necessarily employ'd, to promote the Appetite, and assist Digestion.

In defining woodwinds as improper for female performers, Essex was harking back to the ancient Greeks, who told of Athena's invention of the *aulos*, a recorder-like instrument. Once Athena realized how the instrument "distorted" her face, the myth goes, she threw it aside, not wishing to appear unseemly. This ancient division between "proper" instruments— those that are touched—and "improper" ones—those that are blown—remained prominent during the armonica's heyday. In the late 1700s, the armonica's seemingly gentle and graceful nature placed it in a separate category from "coarse, strenuous" pipe instruments that were suitable for men.

We can see this dynamic in an anecdote from a man named Herr Christmann, who in 1790 visited the music teacher and armonica builder Joseph Aloys Schmittbaur in Germany. During his visit Christmann met a twelve-year-old student of Schmittbaur's named Mlle. George, who, in a parlor performance, played the armonica, Christmann reported, "with much delicacy." Later Christmann attended a performance of regimental music by seven young male students of Schmittbaur's, which took place on the city's public parade ground. As Hadlock notes, Mlle. George's parlor armonica performance represents "the domestic feminine space," while the male band

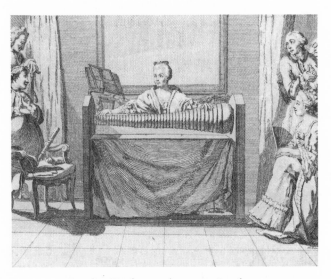

Angelica Kaufmann, glass armonica player.

loudly playing their instruments in a parade concert exemplifies "the public and collective character of masculine musicmaking."

The armonica's foot pedal presented one potentially risky aspect of the instrument for women, as moving the leg up and down could be viewed as overly sensual. To solve this problem, cloth drapery hung from the armonica, concealing the performer's bottom half. For women, the trick, as with any instrument, was to play without *seeming* to play—to "hold a pose," Hadlock writes, that offered "a performance of stillness, balance, and silence." Paintings of female musicians at this time illustrate this ideal, with performers shown touching, but not pressing, their instruments.

For people worried about music's deleterious effect on the nerves, or, in Kennaway's words, the "sheer physical pleasure of musical stimulation," not to mention its "feminine associations," the glass armonica represented the purest example—the material actualization—of their fears. If music in general could now be viewed as potentially dangerous, an unruly force that could whip the passions into a personal and even societal frenzy, then the armonica's unearthly sounds no longer called to mind a heavenly order—instead, they conjured images of chaos and dark disruption in a lower realm.

Even for those less inclined to such hellish imaginings, the armonica's otherworldly connotations, its intimate connections with the nerves, suggested an instrument that was less than purely "musical." Writing in 1810, Samuel Taylor Coleridge argued that the armonica could not please "a true musical taste" because its "crystalline tone" prevented the listener from focusing on what was really important, the synchronized convergence between sound and materials. "The body of the sound . . . or that effect which is derived from the materials," Coleridge wrote, "encroaches too far on the effect from the proportions of the notes, or that which is given to music by the mind." Real music, in other words, needed to satisfy the intellect, which was attuned to the controlled interplay between harmony and rhythm. The armonica's ethereal sounds merely excited one's senses, Coleridge felt, a much more base achievement.

More recent theories have suggested that if people in earlier times *were* in fact driven insane by playing the armonica, it may have been due to lead poisoning caused by the instrument's glass. But as William Zeitler points out, this theory has several holes. To begin with, the eighteenth-century armonicas that we know of were made with soda-lime glass, not lead glass. What's more, contemporary research has shown that lead poisoning does not occur through skin contact—the lead must be ingested or inhaled instead. And while some have argued that armonica players may have licked their fingers to wet the glasses, potentially ingesting lead this way, this theory is almost certainly incorrect, since wetting thirty-seven glasses and keeping them moist over time would have required far more saliva than humans can generate.

Ultimately, the glass armonica's eventual disappearance didn't result solely from some universally agreed upon condemnation of its hazardous powers. Other, more mundane factors were involved in the instrument's decline. One of these was the hefty expense of actually building an armonica—a reality that remains little changed today. Another factor was the fragility of the final product: as we have seen, not only did the instrument's brittle glass frequently break during transport, it sometimes even shattered from the vibrations of its own notes.

A final factor, one that likely would have doomed the armonica to obscurity even if the instrument had *not* been rumored to destroy the nerves, was the changing style of music in the late eighteenth and early nineteenth centuries. This period saw a shift from chamber music, which was performed in small rooms to select audiences, to grand orchestral accompaniments—part of the awakening Romantic spirit—that required large concert halls. Within these roomy new performance spaces, the relatively gentle sounds of the glass armonica simply couldn't be heard. Take this *Morning Chronicle* review of a 1794 concert in London: "The dulcet notes of the instrument would be delightful indeed, were they more powerful and articulate. In a smaller room, and an audience less numerous, the effect must be enchanting. Though the accompaniments were kept very much under, they were still occasionally too loud."

On this last point, we can gain a greater sense of why the glass armonica—a relatively inflexible instrument in regard to volume and playing style—fell out of favor if we compare it with an instrument whose immense adaptability and continual refinement has allowed it to thrive for centuries: the piano. Like the armonica, the piano was built upon the foundation of earlier musical instruments, specifically the dulcimer, the clavichord, and the harpsichord. But while the harpsichord's strings were plucked by quills, and the clavichord's were struck by tangents that stayed in contact with the strings, the piano's key innovation was that its strings were struck by rebounding hammers.

As early as the sixteenth century, there had been efforts to build stringed keyboard instruments with hammering mechanisms. These efforts produced a body of knowledge regarding the best methods for building cases, soundboards, bridges, and keyboards. But a single individual, Bartolomeo Cristofori, invented what we think of as the modern piano. Cristofori was the keeper of instruments at the Medici court in Florence, and he possessed a wealth of knowledge regarding the construction of stringed keyboard instruments, especially harpsichords. Sometime around 1700 Cristofori used this knowledge and experience to push these instruments to the next level. The piano allowed the playing of notes across the whole spectrum of volume, from soft to loud. In fact, Cristofori first named the instrument *gravicembalo col piano e forte*, or "a harpsichord with loudness and softness." The name was eventually shorted to *pianoforte* or *fortepiano*, and then to *piano*. Because the piano was so responsive to the force with which its keys were struck, it allowed for crescendos and decrescendos and the dynamic control of its phrases. The clavichord also responded dynamically to the force of a player's touch, but its tone was not powerful enough for ensemble music; the harpsichord, meanwhile, possessed greater volume but did not respond to changes in touch. Cristofori's invention fixed both of these issues.

Cristofori's great accomplishment in designing the piano was to solve every essential problem involved in building a workable instrument with hammer-struck strings. Previous designers had struggled to create a means by which the hammers would rebound immediately after they damp the strings. (If the hammers stayed on the strings, they would tamp down the vibrations they created.) Cristofori's solution was to build a mechanism, called an escapement, that caused a hammer to fall away from a string even if the key was still pressed. He also added a lever system that increased the speed of the hammers, and a "back check" that caught the hammers after they struck, ensuring that they would not bounce back and hit the strings again. In addition, Cristofori placed slips of wood with dampers at the end of the keys to keep the keys silent between strikes.

Later eighteenth-century inventors further refined Cristofori's remarkable design. The organ builder Gottfried Silbermann developed a pedal that allowed notes to sustain even after a player's fingers had left the keys—the predecessor to a modern piano's sustain pedal. By the end of the century pianists and composers were clamoring for even louder pianos with even greater note-sustaining capabilities. These changes were made possible by the Industrial Revolution, which allowed for the production of stronger piano wire and more exact iron frames. Nor did the changes stop there. Over the next two centuries the

A Cristofori piano from 1726.

piano, though the heart of its design remained the same, continued to evolve to meet the changing demands and tastes of players, composers, and audiences. As it evolved, it occupied an increasing position of prominence across musical genres, and in venues of all sizes.

By way of contrast, Franklin's armonica could not be modified in any significant way that would increase its adaptability. This was not for lack of trying. Over the years several inventors and musicians attempted to modify Franklin's instrument, most particularly by adding a keyboard. Perhaps the most notable of these individuals was Franklin's lawyer friend Francis Hopkinson, a member of the first graduating class of Franklin's College of Philadelphia (now the University of Pennsylvania), and a prominent musician, composer, and teacher in the city. As a teenager, Hopkinson wrote what is now considered to be the first secular American song, "My Days Have Been So Wondrous Free." He was later a hero of the Revolutionary War, a member of the Continental Congress, a signer of the Declaration of Independence, and one of the designers of the American flag. Franklin, for one, thought Hopkinson was "ingenious," and of "good Morals & obliging Disposition."

In a 1786 letter to Thomas Jefferson, then serving as minister to France, Hopkinson mentioned his efforts to amend the glass armonica:

> My spare Time and Attention is at present much engaged in a Project to make the Harmonica or musical Glasses to be played with Kees [keys], like an Organ. I am now far forward in this Scheme and have little Doubt of Success. It has in vain been attempted in France and England. It may therefore seem too adventurous in me to undertake it, but the Door of Experiment is open.

In his response to Hopkinson, arriving six months later, Jefferson's enthusiasm was palpable, even extraordinarily so. "I am very much pleased with your project on the Harmonica and the prospect of your succeeding in the application of keys to it," Jefferson told his friend, who at the time was serving as a judge of the Admiralty Court of Philadelphia. Any notion that this is mere nicety is done away with by the unfeigned keenness of Jefferson's next statement: "It will be the greatest present which has been made to the musical world this century, not excepting the Piano forte." Even if the project was not a full success, Jefferson reasoned, "If it's tone approaches that given by the finger as nearly only as the harpsichord does that of the harp, it will be very valuable." In a separate letter to an English musician friend of his, Jefferson reported on Hopkinson's efforts, saying that while the instrument might not be appropriate for the "general mass of music compositions," it was "delicious" for "those of a certain character."

Both Jefferson's and Hopkinson's gusto was ultimately for naught. In 1787 Hopkinson informed Jefferson that he had finally "succeeded in making the Harmonica to be played with Kees, as far as I believe the Instrument is capable." But this modification would not be a bountiful gift to the musical world after all. The keyboard, Hopkinson reported, "required too much Address in the manner of wetting the Cushions, for common Use." But a relentless inventor like Hopkinson, much like Franklin, wasn't one to mourn his losses. He went on to tell Jefferson that in the course of his experiments on the glass armonica, he "discover'd a method of drawing the Tone from Metal Bells by Friction, to an amazing Perfection, without the necessity of Water or any Fluid." His fervor reignited, Hopkinson announced, "I am getting a Set of Bells cast, and expect to introduce a new musical Instrument to be called the *Bellarmonic*."

Two years before this exchange, Franklin himself received

word from a nobleman in Turin that a fellow Italian had attached a keyboard to the armonica. In his response, Franklin discussed the various roadblocks that other would-be inventors had encountered. Twelve years before, he wrote, an "ingenious" musician in London named Steele had attempted to do the same thing, "but the tones were with difficulty produc'd by the touch from the keys, and the machinery in playing made so much noise and rattle," that Steele had eventually given up. In Paris, the Duchess of Villeroy had undertaken a similar project, but she had yet to produce satisfactory results. At about the same time as the nobleman in Turin had contacted Franklin, a Baron Feriet of Versailles began yet another attempt to add a keyboard to the instrument. Franklin's high opinion of Feriet's intelligence and manual dexterity had led him to believe that Feriet might succeed, but, Franklin regretfully told the Italian nobleman, "I begin to doubt it, as I hear nothing from him lately." Franklin then described his own method of playing the armonica by hand, writing that his fingers were "capable of touching [the glasses] with [such] great delicacy" that no other sounds interfered with the glasses' pure tones. If the keyboard invented by the Italian gentleman had the same "advantages," Franklin politely added, then he would "be glad to know the construction."

The keyboard armonica ultimately failed because, as Franklin pointed out, "the machinery in playing made so much noise and rattle, as to diminish greatly the pleasure given by the sound of the glasses." The armonica's gossamer sound can only be drawn from scraping the fingers directly onto the glasses—that is the instrument's founding premise. As an early-twentieth-century German scholar rather excitedly declared: "One wants the thrill, which the fingertips draw from the glasses." So while Franklin's instrument has been somewhat modified over the centuries, the armonica remains, even today, remarkably true to his original design. It is no coincidence, then, that glass music's twentieth-century revival—the subject to which we now turn—occurred in the immediate wake of the invention of electronic amplification.

9

THE ARMONICA'S
REVIVAL

After about 1830, the glass armonica all but faded from view. Though the Italian composer Gaetano Donizetti planned to employ the armonica during a "mad scene" in his 1835 opera *Lucia di Lammermoor* (he ultimately substituted a different instrument), and German composer Richard Strauss stipulated that the armonica be used in his 1919 work *Die Frau ohne Schatten*, the instrument otherwise lingered in obscurity until 1929, when a German musician named Bruno Hoffmann discovered the musical glasses.

Entranced by glass's unusual sound, Hoffmann developed an instrument that he dubbed the "glass harp," which consisted of custom-designed wineglasses fitted in a wooden case, with a resonance chamber beneath. He searched out the armonica's original music—pieces by Mozart, Rollig, Naumann, Reichardt, and others—and transcribed it for his new instrument, while also encouraging new works by contemporary composers that fit the glass harp's unique sound. Over the several remaining decades of his life, Hoffmann played his instrument on countless television and radio programs and recordings, and in live appearances throughout Europe and the British Isles. He is credited with single-handedly reawakening public interest in the glass armonica, despite the fact that his album *Music for Glass Harmonica* actually features the glass harp.

The next step in the armonica's revival came in 1960, when, on a visit to Paris, German glassblower Gerhard Finkenbeiner encountered the instrument in a museum. The armonica was featured as a curiosity, with a sign stating that it had been invented by Franklin and played by Mozart. As a young boy growing up in a musical family on the German-Swiss border, near where Franz Mesmer was raised, Finkenbeiner had heard stories of the glass armonica's distinctive tones. (The instrument's history was still taught in German schools.) Now, as an adult, and with a glassblower's trained eye, he found the crystal bowls enthralling.

Seeking more knowledge, Finkenbeiner found a book that

explained, in his words, "all the hocus-pocus" about the instrument, "the stories about it having supernatural powers." Though he didn't believe the tales, he was nonetheless hooked. "One day I'm going to make one," he told himself, embarking on a decades-long odyssey to create an armonica of his own.

Finkenbeiner's initial foray into glassblowing had come as a teenager in Germany, when, conscripted into a Nazi bomb factory during World War II, he received training in electronics, while also being apprenticed to a master glassmaker. After the war he went to work for the French navy, where he blew glass for infrared detectors, and maintained a passion for such instruments as the piano and organ. Finkenbeiner's love for music inspired him to experiment endlessly with musical inventions—as when, at the request of a priest friend, he created a two-foot-long glass bell by shaping a vacuum tube around a narrow quartz rod. When the instrument was struck with a small hammer and heavily amplified, its sound resembled that of a church bell. In later years, in his office in Waltham, Massachusetts, Finkenbeiner employed a set of similar bells, made of three glass crosses that turned in an ovenlike metal case, as both a door chime and an alarm. He also made a number of glass carillons.

Finkenbeiner first gleaned an idea of how to make an

armonica while working on a project for IBM. He had developed a busy career as one of a small number of scientific glassblowers in the United States, and his days were filled crafting specialized products for organizations such as Raytheon, MIT, and Harvard. For the IBM job Finkenbeiner was blowing furnace tubes for semiconductors, a process that involved sealing off each tube's end to make a vacuum. As he looked at a pile of leftover ends, he was struck by the realization that each discarded piece looked like a glass armonica cup. "So I started saving these ends," he later recalled, "and after a year I had almost a hundred different cups. They needed to be tuned, of course, but that gave me the start. I made one [armonica], and, when it was done, I was fascinated by the sound. It was so great. And nobody had heard one, because, in the museums, they don't let you touch them."

From this improvised start, Finkenbeiner set to work creating, almost singlehandedly, a new and highly specialized market for the glass armonica. He eventually succeeded, and his scientific glassblowing company, G. Finkenbeiner Inc., of Waltham, Massachusetts, began producing eight to ten of the instruments every year, a tradition that continues into the present day. (Finkenbeiner died in a plane crash in 1999.) While the armonicas that Finkenbeiner Inc. produces are largely the same as their eighteenth-century counterparts, they take advantage of contemporary advances in glass manufacturing abilities and technologies. For example, the spindle in a Finkenbeiner armonica is turned via a 110-volt variable speed electric motor, as opposed to a foot treadle. In addition, the glass used by the company is of a much higher quality than the soda-lime glass used in previous centuries. When, in the 1980s, Finkenbeiner conducted a lengthy trial process to determine which type of glass produced the best armonica sound, he found quartz glass to be far superior to crystal, Pyrex, and traditional household glass. Finkenbeiner Inc.'s armonica bowls are therefore molded from the same glass that the company employs in their regular scientific glassblowing work: semiconductor-grade fused quartz, made up of 100 percent pure silica, considered the world's finest glass.

In an article that Finkenbeiner wrote in 1987 heralding the armonica's "return from obscurity," he outlined the meticulous process by which he built his instruments. First he would

mount lengthy tubes of his chosen glass—larger tubes for the lower notes, smaller tubes for the higher ones—onto an industrial-sized lathe. Then, by both turning and blowing, he would tool the molten glass at temperatures around 2000 degrees Celsius, fabricating a series of elongated spheres along the entire length of the cylinder. Each of these spheres will later be sliced in half to produce two unrefined glass [armonica] bells. After the crude cups are made from the glass cylinder, they are classified according to the note each is closest to in pitch. This is accomplished by holding each glass loosely in one's hand in front of an electronic musical stroboscope and then rapping it sharply with a stick to make it ring in its particular frequency.

To avoid the time-consuming practice of fashioning notes one by one to their precise shape and pitch, Finkenbeiner continued using his "random-method approach," producing "hundreds of cups of all shapes, sizes, and tonal qualities." Twelve months' work of this kind would produce around five hundred raw cups, at which point Finkenbeiner would begin the meticulous work of modifying and perfecting the cups to precise concert pitch. If a note proved too flat, he would grind the cup's base to reduce its mass, which would sharpen the pitch. For notes that were too sharp, he used a technique called "acid etching"—literally bathing the cup in hydrofluoric acid—to reduce the thickness of the cup's walls. Once Finkenbeiner had crafted the perfect cups, the final step, mounting them onto a spindle, proved relatively easy.

Finkenbeiner remains the world's leading armonica builder, with everyone from Neil Young to the Sultan of Oman employing its services. (The sultan bought his armonica as a lavish wedding present for a musically gifted bride.) One December morning in 2013, I placed my own order with Diane Hession, the company's office manager, for an F-25C model instrument, a two-octave, 25-note (C5 to C7) armonica that, with a hefty price tag of $8,150 (case included), is the company's *least* expensive model.

But even if several people purchase armonicas every year, only a tiny number of individuals worldwide are considered experts on the instrument. Of these, the world's foremost virtuoso is almost certainly Dennis James, whose glass armonica collaborations with Linda Ronstadt over six CDs during the 1990s and early 2000s helped introduce the instrument to a wider audience. James's introduction to the armonica came at the age of six, when he encountered Benjamin Franklin's original instrument on display in the entry rotunda of the Franklin Institute in

Philadelphia (that particular instrument has since been moved elsewhere). Years later, as a student at Indiana University's Jacobs School of Music, a chance mention of the armonica by one of his professors brought the memory flooding back. "What does it sound like?" James asked his professor. "No one knows," the professor replied. "It hasn't been played for two hundred years."

This exchange kicked off a lengthy effort on James's part to track down a real-life armonica. Eventually he found Bruno Hoffmann's 1963 recording of armonica music, but on a subsequent visit to Switzerland to meet Hoffmann in person, he was dismayed to learn that the German native had used a glass harp, not an armonica, on the record. Hoffmann did, in fact, own a glass armonica, but he told James that it was only "a figment of historical imagination" that the instrument could produce sounds. James, however, couldn't help himself. When Hoffmann left the room to get a drink, James wet his finger and rubbed it along the edge of one of the instrument's glass bowls. A soft, high-pitched sound rose into the air. Hearing it, Hoffmann rushed in from the other room and slapped James's hand. Despite this censure, James's interest in the instrument only increased.

By then it was the early 1980s, and the only available instrument James could locate sold for $1.5 million, which was far beyond his means. Seeking an alternative, he reached out to specialists in the glassmaking capital of Corning, New York, and to their counterparts in Europe and Japan. When this eventually led him to Gerhard Finkenbeiner in Massachusetts, James's problem seemed solved. Yet even after Finkenbeiner built him an armonica, it took James more than a year to draw a sound from it. As it happened, a mistake had occurred during the glassmaking process: gas had thickened into overly dense molecules that left an unseen glaze over the bowls. Thanks to James's persistence, however, a year's worth of failed attempts at playing eventually wore through this outside layer. To James's great surprise and relief, one day his armonica finally "chirped."

Thus began a multiyear odyssey to master his newly functioning instrument. James sought out original eighteenth-century glass music tutorials, consulted with experts in early music, and plunged into the extensive repertoire that had been composed for the armonica during its heyday. In time he discovered twelve different parts of his fingers, along with various hand positions, that affected the armonica's timbre and the speed of its response. The fact that James is double-jointed, and can fold his fingers backward nearly in half, only increased his versatility.

In the late 1980s, finally satisfied with his level of proficiency,

James mailed around a publicity packet that included recordings and a firm declaration: "The armonica is back." Though he didn't ask for jobs, they came to him anyway, and in 1988 he made his debut armonica performance, accompanying players from the New York Philharmonic at a *Vanity Fair* party in Versailles. His armonica career took off so quickly that, in just three years, he had played almost two hundred concerts worldwide. The bicentennial of Mozart's death in 1991 provided James with so much work that he aroused the suspicion of the IRS, who wanted to know how his income had jumped from $12,000 to $250,000 in a mere twelve months.

A 1993 call from Linda Ronstadt, who had long harbored an interest in the sounds of rubbed glass, increased James's armonica profile even further. Beginning with that year's *Winter Light* record, he collaborated with Ronstadt on six more projects, including his own album, *Cristal: Glass Music Through the Ages*, which Ronstadt co-produced. James also gained entry into the lucrative world of film scoring, which brought the armonica further attention.

More recently, in 2010, James was tapped to head the world's first known glass music studies program, at Rutgers University's Mason Gross School of the Arts. Every week, James drives eleven hours round-trip from his home in Corning to teach a single student. His first student was a singer who hoped that playing the armonica would increase his chances of success in the professional world. This is what James and the school's dean envision for the future, a studio rife with glass musicians arming themselves with specialized skills for the cutthroat realities of a life in music.

When I visited James at his grand Victorian house outside Corning, we sat on antique chairs amid his sprawling collection of three hundred rare and historic instruments: not only his beautifully designed $107,000 armonica, custom built by the Eisch glass house in Germany, but also harpsichords, clavichords, pianos, a theremin, a harp, a serpent (a bass wind instrument shaped like its namesake), and numerous others. Here, over cups of tea, James explained to me the pleasures of playing eighteenth-century music on the armonica, beginning with his interest in what he calls "common practice." (In music history, the common practice period lasted for three centuries, from around 1600 to 1900.)

If you think of, say, jazz, when you sit down to play with a jazz ensemble, there's a certain common practice of volume, touch, phrasing, even what notes and how many notes you should play. And these things aren't notated, they're not in any written music, you can only learn them from playing. If you're playing with other musicians, you're learning the language, the "common practice" language. But with eighteenth-century music, we're so far from it, and there obviously weren't any recordings. So you have to deal strictly with what the composers wrote, and the students and critics of the composers wrote.

This is where James's self-described "obsession" stems from. After years—decades, in fact—of studying the armonica, and the eighteenth-century music composed for it, he finally felt that he had gained enough evidence to start homing in on the original "common practices." The new sense of conviction that flowed through his playing was, for him, extraordinary and addictive.

When you gather enough knowledge and understanding, when you've done all the research, you come up with your own assessments of how things must have been. And when you convince *yourself*, it's a glorious thing, almost unequaled in music. When you're comfortable enough in your understanding that the music *erupts* out of these common practice applications, and you satisfy *yourself*, there's nothing like it.

This feeling, however, doesn't mean that you are objectively correct. As James points out, "You might change in six weeks, you might see something that you didn't see before, and you might refine your own understanding." But that, he says, is the whole "joy and game" of it: "You're not trying to pass some examination with somebody standing next to you who might know more than you. Instead, it's the utter conviction that while you're doing it, it feels right."

James isn't the only musician who has helped bring the armonica's sounds to a wider contemporary audience. The French musician Thomas Bloch, who teaches ondes Martenot at the Strasbourg Conservatory, has played his glass armonica with a roster of some of the rock world's most innovative artists, including Radiohead, Tom Waits, Daft Punk, Damon Albarn, Imogen Heap, and Patrick Wolf. He has also played on hundreds of film, television, and radio projects. Like James, Bloch first heard of the glass armonica by way of Bruno Hoffmann, and he bought his first instrument from Gerhard Finkenbeiner.

Dennis James playing his glass armonica.

But the range of Bloch's experiences with the armonica are fairly unique in the world today. "I play Mozart one day and thrash rock the day after," he says, and he is an equally experienced performer of classical, opera, pop, world music, and avant-garde music.

But how does one even begin to *learn* to play the glass armonica, let alone become a virtuoso? Aside from the instruction Dennis James provides in Rutgers's glass music program, there are no armonica teachers, at least as far as I've been able to determine. And YouTube videos of the glass armonica are less helpful than they might seem, because professional players make the task of drawing sounds from the instrument appear deceptively easy, as if they are barely touching the rims of the glass bowls. In reality it can take weeks or months to achieve even the tiniest squeak, as the armonica expert William Zeitler told me from his own experience—and as I've experienced in my own efforts to learn the instrument. So, fine, it's the old Carnegie Hall joke writ large, but if one is looking for a little guidance to get started, the best place to look, as Gerhard Finkenbeiner and Dennis James did, is at the original eighteenth- and nineteenth-century method books, rare as they might be: Franz Konrad Bartl's *About the Keyed Armonica*, James Smith's *Tutor for the Musical Glasses*,

J. E. Franklin's *Introduction to the Knowledge of the Seraphim or Musical Glasses*, Francis Hopkinson Smith's *Tutor for the Grand Harmonicon*. When I received my armonica from Finkenbeiner Inc., they included Johann Christian Müller's guide, *A Self-Instruction Manual for the Glass Harmonica*, originally published in Leipzig in 1788. Müller's manual provides sensible guidance for the conditions required to play the armonica, as well. The room, for example, "should be neither too warm nor too cold. If it is too warm, the bells—under warm hands—begin to whistle and squeak, on the other hand, if it is too cold, they may not produce any sound at all."

The most readily available method book, and probably the most welcoming, is Ann Ford's groundbreaking *Instructions for Playing on the Musical Glasses*, which, as we learned in Chapter 1, she published in November 1761. (Thomas Jefferson kept a copy in his library.) She wrote the brief book a mere four weeks after she first heard the musical glasses, which makes her title page reassurance—that "Any Person, who has the least Knowledge of Music, or a good ear, may be able to perform in a few Days, if not in a few Hours"—seem all the more plausible.

To play the glass armonica, the first step, as Benjamin Franklin noted, is to wash one's fingers thoroughly to remove all

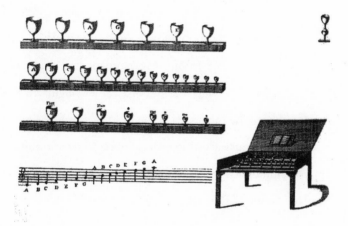

Ann Ford's *Instructions for Playing on the Musical Glasses*, 1761.

possible traces of oil. William Zeitler and Dennis James recommend spending a full ten minutes on this task. James, for one, also cleans his armonica every time he plays, using alcohol and 100 percent cotton pads. Part of this, he says, is about ritual, which he believes is crucial when you're approaching an instrument. Every time he sits down to play the armonica, for example, he starts with Mozart's Adagio in C Major, widely acknowledged as the finest piece ever composed for the instrument. This helps James "get into the head space" of the instrument, and remember all the refinements of playing it. Ann Ford, rather singularly, recommends rubbing the fingers with the pulp of an unripe grape before playing the musical glasses; some contemporary armonica players use lemon juice or alcohol in addition to water and soap. With this accomplished, Ford writes,

> to produce the tone clearly and properly from the smaller treble glasses, the ball of the middle fingers, or the prominent part between the first and second joint, being wet, must be flatly, and regularly moved, in a circular motion, on the top of the glasses; but this touch will not do for the large triple octaves, which are apt (from their great vibration) to give false tones, if so touched; and therefore these are to be touched

with the ball of the fore, or middle finger, about half an inch below the rim on the outside; and by a very little practice, the glasses will, by their greater or less vibration, inform the practitioner how the touch is to be applied to produce the true tone.

Crucial to playing the armonica is to recognize that "rubbing" the glass bowls isn't the most accurate description. The process is more of a quick catch-and-release, like how a violin bow strikes the strings. As Johann Christian Müller's guide notes, playing the armonica is not like playing the piano, for which one uses a "horizontally curved finger." Instead, armonica players should employ "long outstretched fingers. Playing should not be accomplished with the fingertips, as some incorrectly believe, but with the inner and outer joints of the fingers of both hands." (This explains why Dennis James's double-jointedness helps makes him such an effective player.)

Müller writes further that "it is necessary to stroke the bells as gently as possible with the fingers in the direction opposite that of the rotation. The good and characteristic tone is not achieved by sudden pressure, but by touching the bells gently." In Dennis James's evocative phrase, it is like stroking a lover's eyelash—*just* the eyelash. This is the process that can take so long for beginners to master, a delicate balance of softness and steadiness that, at first blush, can seem counterintuitive.

But the rewards—one thinks back to the words that repeat seemingly endlessly in the glass armonica's history: "ethereal," "haunting," "heavenly." Or, depending on your musical taste, maybe simply "eerie" or "unusual." As Johann Christian Müller writes in his manual, "The almost inaudible beginning of the tone, its increase and vanishing, which are so natural to this and no other instrument, are the most specifically characteristic features of the armonica." Both beginning and advanced players, he urges, "should combine tones only in order to stimulate those unexpected sensations that no instrument under the sun offers in such full measure." One doesn't have to be Benjamin Franklin's wife, Deborah, waking up to the strange new sounds of her husband playing his armonica in the attic, and immediately convinced "that she had died and gone to heaven and was listening to the music of the angels," to be struck by the power of something utterly unique.

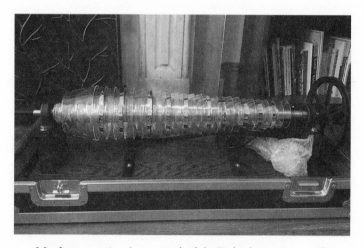

My glass armonica. Armonicas built by Finkenbeiner Inc. weigh between 35 and 45 pounds, with price tags beginning at $7,500.

ACKNOWLEDGMENTS

A number of people have provided essential help, advice, and support during the writing of this book. Among those I would like to acknowledge and thank are:

Melanie Jackson, agent.

My deservedly legendary editor, Alice Mayhew; her fantastic assistant, Stuart Roberts; and the rest of the team at Simon & Schuster.

William Zeitler, glass armonica player and author, without whose groundbreaking research this book could not have been written. His book, *The Glass Armonica: The Music and the Madness*, is vital reading.

Dennis James, a true musical virtuoso.

My friends and colleagues.

My amazing family.

Laura and Caleb, for everything.

NOTES

INTRODUCTION

xix *In the 1740s*: Ellen R. Cohn, "Benjamin Franklin and Traditional Music," in *Reappraising Benjamin Franklin*, J. A. L. Lemay, ed. (Newark: University of Delaware Press, 1993), 290.

xxi *The armonica appeared at a time*: Paul Johnson, *Mozart* (New York: Penguin, 2013).

xxii *For a period of time in the late eighteenth century*: Heather Hadlock, "Sonorous Bodies: Women and the Glass Harmonica," *Journal of the American Musicological Society* 53, no. 3 (2000): 507.

xxii *"Like Orpheus's lyre"*: Ibid., 507–8.

xxii *A large glass armonica factory*: Gerhard Finkenbeiner and Vera Meyer, "The Glass Harmonica: A Return from Obscurity," *Leonardo* 20, no. 2 (1987): 139–42.

xxii   *With the onset of the nineteenth century, the armonica*: Hadlock, "Sonorous Bodies," 508.

xxii   *Take the author, composer, and music critic*: Ibid.

1: THE ANGELICK ORGAN

3   *Those who admired him*: E. Power Biggs, "Benjamin Franklin and the Armonica," *Daedalus* 86, no. 3 (1957): 231–41.

3   *Benjamin Franklin knew of him, noting*: *The Papers of Benjamin Franklin*, ed. Leonard Labaree et al. (New Haven: Yale University Press, 1959), To Beccaria, July 13, 1762. Hereafter *PBF.*

4   *Pockrich's father, a member of Parliament*: David O'Donoghue, "An Irish Musical Genius," 13–14. See also William Zeitler, *The Glass Armonica: The Music and the Madness* (Musica Arcana, 2013), 58.

4   *As a young man, Richard inherited*: O'Donoghue, "An Irish Musical Genius," 14; Zeitler, *The Glass Armonica*, 59.

5   *He also disgorged a good part*: Zeitler, *The Glass Armonica*, 60.

5   *"Take common brown paper"*: Ibid.

5   *As it happens, his method*: Brian Boydell, "Mr. Pockrich

and the Musical Glasses," *Dublin Historical Record* 44, no. 2 (1991): 25–33.

5 *If given the necessary money*: Ibid., 17.

5 *The pumped-in blood*: John Carteret Pilkington, *The Real Story of John Carteret Pilkington* (1760), 132–33.

6 *"anyone attaining the age of 999 years"*: O'Donoghue, "An Irish Musical Genius," 14; Zeitler, *The Glass Armonica* 59.

6 *This would ensure that relatives*: Boydell, "Mr. Pockrich and the Musical Glasses," 17.

6 *At a time when ships*: Zeitler, *The Glass Armonica*, 61.

6 *In the realm of the arts*: O'Donoghue, "An Irish Musical Genius," 16; Zeitler, *The Glass Armonica*.

6 *Improvising upon a long tradition*: David Gallo and Stanley Finger, "The Power of a Musical Instrument," *History of Psychology*, 3, no. 4 (2000): 328.

7 *For many female performers*: Boydell "Mr. Pockrich and the Musical Glasses."

7 *"At the Theatre in Smock-Alley"*: Ibid.

8 *Three different times, he and his mother*: Zeitler, *The Glass Armonica*, 68.

8 *The Captain cut quite a figure*: Biggs, "Benjamin Franklin and the Armonica."

8 *As the two began chatting*: Pilkington, *The Real Story of John Carteret Pilkington*, 57.

8 *With typical modesty*: Ibid., 58.

9 *Cheered by Pilkington's hearty applause*: Ibid., 58–59.

10 *Ever shameless, and talking*: Ibid., 59.

10 *Noting Pilkington's look of dismay*: Ibid., 60.

11 *In a further attempt to reassure*: Ibid., 61.

11 *Once their repertoire was settled*: Ibid., 66.

11 *Three hours before the concert's kickoff*: Ibid., 66–67.

12 *He rebuilt his angelick organ*: William H. Grattan Flood, "XXV. Handel and Arne in Ireland," *A History of Irish Music*, 1905.

12 *One year later, Pockrich, a bachelor*: Boydell "Mr. Pockrich and the Musical Glasses."

12 *As for Pockrich, the highlight*: Biggs, "Benjamin Franklin and the Armonica," 233.

13 *In November 1759, in the midst*: O'Donoghue, "An Irish Musical Genius."

14 *"Old Pock, no more, still lives"*: Biggs, "Benjamin Franklin and the Armonica," 233–34.

15 *"nine cups, struck with a stick"*: A. Hyatt King, "The Musical

Glasses and Glass Armonica," *Proceedings of the Royal Musical Association* 72 (1946–47): 97.

15 *A Japanese contemporary*: Ibid.

15 *Two centuries later*: Ibid., 98.

15 *One passage describes*: Ibid.

16 *The book features a woodcut*: Gallo and Finger, "The Power of a Musical Instrument," 327.

16 *More than 150 years later*: King, "The Musical Glasses and Glass Armonica," 99.

16 *In 1627, Francis Bacon*: Zeitler, *The Glass Armonica*, 44–45.

18 *Galileo wrote* Two New Sciences: Ibid., 45.

18 *"a glass of water may be made to emit"*: Galileo Galilei, *Two New Sciences*, 1638.

19 *"you wet your index finger"*: Athanasius Kircher, *Phonurgia Nova*, 1673.

19 *The first European mention of musical glasses*: King, "The Musical Glasses and Glass Armonica," 99.

20 *According to the booklet, the vérillon*: Ibid., 100–110.

20 *Any "musical glass" or "singing glass"*: Zeitler, *The Glass Armonica*, 39–41.

21 *A doted-upon only child, Ann*: Peter Holman, "Ann Ford Revisited," in *Eighteenth Century Music* (Cambridge University Press, 2004), 160.

23 *"attracted the notice of all the gay and fashionable world"*: Holman, "Ann Ford Revisited," 162.

23 *Often she was accompanied by*: Ibid., 164–65.

23 *"They introduced a procession of vestals"*: Ibid., 168.

24 *The premises were soon surrounded*: Ibid., 170.

25 *"every one was eager to subscribe"*: Ibid.

25 *Ann's musical talents weren't the only appeal*: Simon McVeigh, *Concert Life in London from Mozart to Haydn* (Cambridge: Cambridge University Press, 1993).

25 *Her embarrassed father offered her*: Michael Rosenthal, "Thomas Gainsborough's Ann Ford," *The Art Bulletin* 80, no. 4 (1998): 649–65.

25 *Angered by his daughter's rebelliousness*: Holman, "Ann Ford Revisited," 171.

26 *"Return, O God of Hosts"*: Ibid.

27 *By far the grandest project*: Rosenthal, "Thomas Gainsborough's Ann Ford."

27 *"Miss Ford's picture, a whole length"*: Holman, "Ann Ford Revisited," 157.

27 *Joseph Burke writes of how*: Zeitler, *The Glass Armonica*.

27 *After nine months in Bath*: Holman, "Ann Ford Revisited," 173.

29 *"a pupil of Schumann"*: Ibid.

29 *Ann's concerts at the Auction House*: Ibid., 175.

29 *"daily exhibition performances"*: McVeigh, "Concert Life in London from Mozart to Haydn."

30 *"every Day upon the GLASSES"*: Holman, "Ann Ford Revisited," 174.

30 *On November 2, 1761*: Ibid.

30 *"As the Tones of the Musical Glasses"*: Ann Ford, *Instructions for Playing on the Musical Glasses* (London: *Public Advertiser*, 1761).

31 *When at long last his grief abated*: Zeitler, *The Glass Armonica*, 87.

32 *"notorious as an ardent supporter"*: Ibid.

32 *"elegant, delicate, powerful woman"*: Holman, "Ann Ford Revisited," 176.

32 *"in many respects the most singular"*: Ibid., 158.

32 *After spending her last years*: Zeitler, *The Glass Armonica*, 92.

2: BENJAMIN FRANKLIN AND MUSIC

35 *He was a capable player of several musical instruments*: Cohn, "Benjamin Franklin and Traditional Music," 291–92.

36 *He derided the "fiddling man"*: Zeitler, *The Glass Armonica*.

36 *"existed in a social context"*: Cohn, "Benjamin Franklin and Traditional Music," 292.

37 *For this reason, his preferred locale*: Ibid.

37 *The Franklin family's gift for music*: Ibid., 294.

38 *Sally wasn't the only younger family member*: Ibid., 294–95.

38 *For an eighteenth-century male of Franklin's*: Helen Cripe, *Thomas Jefferson and Music* (Charlottesville: University of Virginia Press, rev. ed., 2010.)

39 *Part of Franklin's investigation of the essence*: Cohn, "Benjamin Franklin and Traditional Music," 312–13.

40 *"the pleasure derived from watching"*: Ibid., 295.

40 *British writers of the time*: McVeigh, "Concert Life in London from Mozart to Haydn," 129–30.

41 *In a letter to his royal friend Lord Kames*: Cohn, "Benjamin Franklin and Traditional Music," 295.

42 *"had a functional as well as"*: Ibid., 296.

43 *Franklin followed his own advice*: Ibid., 292.

43 *Franklin wrote his first two published songs*: Ibid., 297.

43 *Regardless, his no-nonsense father Josiah*: Ibid., 300.

44 *Around 1765, Franklin penned*: Ibid., 305–6.

45 *"As they could not get before us"*: Ibid., 307.

45 *Franklin's songs are a vivid expression*: Ibid., 315.

45 *Even into his last months*: Ibid., 316.

46 *"It seems a long time since I heard from you"*: Ibid.

3: BENJAMIN FRANKLIN AND THE INVENTION OF THE ARMONICA

49 *In the decades before the American Revolution*: Walter Isaacson, *Benjamin Franklin: An American Life* (New York: Simon & Schuster, 2003), 155.

50 *If Penn refused his entreaties*: Ibid., 173.

50 *At the time of Franklin's arrival*: Ibid., 181.

51 *He'd also received honorary degrees*: Edmund Morgan, *Benjamin Franklin* (New Haven: Yale University Press, 2002), 107.

51 *His new friends were printers*: Isaacson, *Benjamin Franklin*, 181.

51 *At the time, London offered*: McVeigh, "Concert Life in London from Mozart to Haydn," xiv.

52 *Perhaps the most significant concert*: Zeitler, *The Glass Armonica*, 96.

52 *"We heard Delaval the other night"*: Ibid.

53 *"charmed with the sweetness"*: PBF, To Beccaria, July 13, 1762.

53 *"to see the glasses disposed"*: Ibid.

53 *"Franklin's genius generally consisted in"*: H. W. Brands, *The First American: The Life and Times of Benjamin Franklin* (New York: Doubleday, 2000), 324.

54 *"As we enjoy great Advantages"*: Benjamin Franklin, *The Autobiography of Benjamin Franklin*, 55.

55 *"a kind of sandals"*: Benjamin Franklin, *Memoirs of Benjamin Franklin*, vol. 2, 383.

55 *"For a new appearance"*: PBF, To J. Pringle, December 1, 1762.

56 *"fit the pattern"*: Brands, *The First American*, 324.

56 *"the electric genius"*: PBF, To Beccaria, July 13, 1762, footnote.

57 *Franklin set down specific guidelines*: PBF, To Beccaria, July 13, 1762.

57 *Franklin went into exhaustive detail*: Ibid.

57 *Franklin did not invent this particular*: Zeitler, *The Glass Armonica*, 115.

58 *In a later letter, Franklin gave detailed instructions*: PBF, "Some Directions for Drawing Out the Tone from the Glasses of the Armonica," year unknown.

60 *"The celebrated glassy-chord"*: PBF, To Beccaria, July 13, 1762, footnote.

60 *One scholar hypothesizes that Franklin's*: Antonio Pace, *Benjamin Franklin and Italy* (Philadelphia: American Philosophical Society, 1958), 268–83.

62 *Nearly from the start, however*: Gallo and Finger, "The Power of a Musical Instrument."

62 *"The Armonica. Being the musical glasses"*: King, "The Musical Glasses and Glass Armonica," 107–8.

63 *"the maker who has been employed"*: PBF, To Hughes and Co.: Directions for Making a Musical Instrument, 1762, footnote.

63 *"may be so constructed"*: PBF, To Beccaria, July 13, 1762, footnote.

63 *"I am vex'd with Mr. James"*: PBF, To Polly Stevenson, March 25, 1763.

64 *"the price of a good harmonica"*: Papers of Thomas Jefferson, To John Trumbull, October 11, 1787.

64 *"musical performances on glasses"*: Pace, *Benjamin Franklin and Italy*, 273.

64 *"The two ladies . . . would talk of nothing but"*: Zeitler, *The Glass Armonica.*

65 *"a tune on the Armonica"*: Ibid.

65 *As Franklin began to play*: Ibid.

65 *"gilt carvings, an ornamental fireplace"*: Benjamin Franklin's "Good House," Interior Department, National Park Service, 26.

65 *"I play some of the softest Tunes"*: PBF, To Beccaria, July 13, 1762.

66 *When Princess Izabella Czartoryska*: Z. J. Lipowski, "Benjamin Franklin as a Psychotherapist: A Forerunner of Brief Psychotherapy," *Perspectives in Biology and Medicine* 27 (1984): 362.

67 *"perfectly at ease in his presence"*: PBF, From Elkanah Watson's Diary, November 19, 1781.

4: A BRIEF HISTORY OF GLASS

74 *"more to the Romans than the Victorians"*: Alan Macfarlane and Gerry Martin, *Glass: A World History* (Chicago: University of Chicago Press, 2002).

75 *"glass-soaked"*: Ibid.

75 *"the ability to extend"*: Ibid.

76 *"transparent streams flowing forth"*: Ibid.

76 *The Romans of Pliny's time*: David Whitehouse, *Glass: A Short History* (Washington, DC: Smithsonian Books, 2012).

81 *"if the letters of a book"*: Ibid.

83 *"exploded like a magnificent display"*: Ibid.

86 *"the most effective innovation in glassmaking"*: Ibid.

89 *"a revolution in communications"*: Ibid.

5: AN INSTRUMENT SO GRAND AND HAUNTED

93 *Keyboard instruments like the harpsichord*: Cripe, *Thomas Jefferson and Music*, 43–44.

94 *"to move an audience through"*: Richard Taruskin, *The Oxford History of Western Music*, vol. 2. (Oxford: Oxford University Press, 2005), 460.

94 *Perhaps the greatest expression*: Ibid., 451.

94 *"For many years one has imagined"*: Ibid.

95 *A sweepingly popular "back to nature"*: Donald J. Grout and Claude Palisca, *A History of Western Music* (New York: W. W. Norton, 5th ed., 1996), 443.

96 *"a new imaginative intensity"*: Richard Holmes, *The Age of Wonder* (New York: Vintage, 2010), xvi.

96 *"a softer 'dynamic' science"*: Ibid, xx.

96 *During this transformational period*: Grout and Palisca, *A History of Western Music*, 443–44.

97 *Stylistically, the musical period between*: Julian Rushton, *Classical Music: A Concise History from Gluck to Beethoven* (London: Thames & Hudson, 1986), 9.

98 *It suggests humanism as opposed to*: Grout and Palisca, *A History of Western Music*.

98 *And though the musical forms of the period*: Rushton, *Classical Music*, 10.

98 *"wildly exposed"*: Dennis James, personal interview.

99 *"The masses and oratorios of Haydn"*: Rushton, *Classical Music.*

99 *Marianne was a youth prodigy*: Betty Matthews, "The Davies Sisters, J. C. Bach and the Glass Harmonica," *Music and Letters* 56, no. 2 (April 1975): 150–69.

100 *"whom the inventor has endowed"*: Zeitler, *The Glass Armonica*, 132.

101 *By 1767, Marianne's younger sister Cecilia*: Matthews, "The Davies Sisters, J. C. Bach and the Glass Armonica."

101 *According to Franklin's friend*: Zeitler, *The Glass Armonica*, 132.

101 *With an eye toward increasing*: Matthews, "The Davies Sisters, J. C. Bach and the Glass Armonica."

102 *"has with her a newly invented instrument"*: Ibid., 154.

102 *And indeed, the sisters ultimately*: Ibid.

103 *For the occasion, the court poet*: Zeitler, *The Glass Armonica*, 134.

103 *Apparently the performance was a great success*: Matthews, "The Davies Sisters, J. C. Bach and the Glass Armonica."

104 *"hardly express their joy"*: Ibid.

105 *"I have the honor of presenting"*: Ibid.

106 *"I hope you will excuse the liberty I take"*: PBF, To Benjamin Franklin from Cecilia Davies, January 29, 1778.

106 *"almost too much for us to bear"*: PBF, To Benjamin Franklin from Mary Ann Davies, April 26, 1783.

109 *"so unfortunate as never to have had"*: PBF, To Benjamin Franklin from Mary Ann Davies, October 17, 1783.

109 *"original plàyer of the instrument of electrical music"*: Zeitler *The Glass Armonica*.

110 *"Every December"*: Ibid.

110 *"But allass! I must now"*: Matthews, "The Davies Sisters, J. C. Bach, and the Glass Armonica," 168.

110 *"is still in good order"*: Ibid.

111 *The armonica's other eighteenth-century virtuoso*: Zeitler, *The Glass Armonica*.

112 *"famous blind virtuosa"*: Ibid., 162.

113 *"associated each instrument with particular people"*: Johnson, *Mozart*.

113 *A piece for armonica, viola, flute, cello*: Horace Ervin "Notes on Franklin's Armonica and the Music Mozart Wrote for It," *Journal of the Franklin Institute* 262 (1956), 342.

113 *As Kirchgessner wrote*: Zeitler, *The Glass Armonica*, 163.

114 *There are no records of whether*: Ervin, "Notes on Franklin's Armonica and the Music Mozart wrote for It."

114 *Either way, the composer began writing*: Zeitler, *The Glass Armonica.*

114 *"dulcet tones"*: Ibid.

116 *"Ha, a strange sunshine radiates"*: Ibid.

117 *"Although she was barely able to see"*: Ibid.

117 *"destroyed" by the death*: Ibid.

118 *Born in Hamburg around 1750*: The New Grove Dictionary of Music and Musicians, "Röllig, Karl Leopold."

119 *"subtle use of diminished and augmented"*: Ibid.

119 *Röllig's real fame, however*: Zeitler, *The Glass Armonica.*

120 *"the most beautiful and pleasant instrument"*: Ibid.

6: THE ARMONICA IN
GERMANY AND AMERICA

125 *"Everyone knows that the armonica created"*: Zeitler, *The Glass Armonica.*

126 *"Youngest and fairest of the four"*: Ibid.   .

127 *"totally obsessed"*: E. T. A. Hoffmann's Musical Writings,

D. Charlton, ed. (Cambridge: Cambridge University Press, 1989), 418–19.

130 *The instrument's first recorded American performance*: Zeitler, *The Glass Armonica*.

131 *Almost all of the music in America at that time*: Cripe, *Thomas Jefferson and Music*, 13–14.

7: MESMER AND THE ARMONICA

135 *"the most celebrated, notorious, adulated"*: Vincent Buranelli, *The Wizard from Vienna* (New York: Coward, McCann & Geoghegan, 1975), 15.

135 *Mesmer was born in the tree-shaded*: Ibid.

136 *Mesmer's father worked as*: Frank A. Pattie, *Mesmer and Animal Magnetism: A Chapter in the History of Medicine* (Hamilton, NY: Edmonston Publishing, 1994).

136 *But Mesmer's interest lay less*: Buranelli, *The Wizard from Vienna*.

137 *In keeping with these reforms*: Pattie, *Mesmer and Animal Magnetism*.

137 *The latest findings in anatomy*: Buranelli, *The Wizard from Vienna*.

139 *But his favorite instrument was a recent*: Pattie, *Mesmer and Animal Magnetism.*

139 *Every week Mesmer held an open*: Buranelli, *The Wizard from Vienna.*

141 *"Nobody recognized Wolfgang"*: Ibid., 55.

141 *"How I should like to have one!"*: Gallo and Finger, "The Power of a Musical Instrument," 333.

141 *"extremely fine, with views"*: Buranelli, "The Wizard from Vienna," 56.

142 *"Here and there a touch"*: Ibid., 57.

143 *"universal fluid"*: Ibid.

144 *"The magnetic influence"*: Ibid.

144 *"Almost immediately"*: Ibid.

145 *"obstruction of the flow of animal magnetism"*: Pattie, "Mesmer and Animal Magnetism."

145 *He had, in effect, hypnotized*: Buranelli, "The Wizard from Vienna."

146 *"I hear . . . the Vienna conjuror"*: Gallo and Finger, "The Power of a Musical Instrument," 335–36.

146 *Mesmer responded to his critics*: Buranelli, "The Wizard from Vienna."

147 *"all this nonsense"*: Ibid.

149 *Here he began to perfect*: Gallo and Finger, "The Power of a Musical Instrument."

150 *At times the only sound was the heavy*: Zeitler, *The Glass Armonica*.

150 *"communicated, propagated, and reinforced"*: Gallo and Finger, "The Power of a Musical Instrument."

151 *"After several turns around the room"*: Ibid., 337.

151 *In 1779 he played for the famous*: Ibid.

153 *They declared his cases inconclusive*: Buranelli, "The Wizard from Vienna."

153 *He invited Benjamin Franklin*: Gallo and Finger, "The Power of a Musical Instrument."

154 *In effect, it was a secret society*: Buranelli, "The Wizard from Vienna."

155 *"I cannot but fear that the expectation"*: PBF, To de la Condamine. March 19, 1784.

155 *That same year, Louis XVI*: Buranelli. "The Wizard from Vienna."

156 *"told some [patients] that nonmagnetized"*: Gallo and Finger, "The Power of a Musical Instrument," 339.

157 *"nothing proves the existence"*: Ibid., 340.

157   *"all group treatment where the methods"*: Buranelli, "The Wizard from Vienna," 163.

157   *"Mesmer continues . . . and still has some"*: PBF, To Ingenhousz, April 29, 1785.

158   *He continued to play extensively*: Buranelli, "The Wizard from Vienna."

8: THE ARMONICA FADES
INTO OBSCURITY

162   *"melancholy timbre of the armonica"*: Zeitler, *The Glass Armonica.*

162   *"nervously infirm should not attempt"*: Ibid.

163   *"a great degree of nervous weakness"*: Ibid.

164   *"piercing and penetrating"*: Ibid.

167   *"If playing the armonica were to bring"*: Ibid.

168   *Medical experts and philosophers alike*: James Kennaway, *Bad Vibrations: The History of the Idea of Music as a Cause of Disease* (Burlington, VT: Ashgate, 2012).

169   *"tremulous Motions of the Air"*: Ibid., 26–27.

170   *"If music be the food of love"*: Ibid., 31.

170 *"violently agitated"*: Ibid.

171 *"medical and moral effects on women"*: Ibid., 44.

171 *"represented as a 'sister'"*: Hadlock, "Sonorous Bodies," 508.

171 *"to hear women making music"*: Ibid., 511.

172 "The Harpsichord, Spinet, Lute": Ibid., 510.

173 *"coarse, strenuous"*: Ibid.

173 *"the domestic feminine space"*: Ibid., 510.

175 *"hold a pose"*: Ibid., 511.

175 *"sheer physical pleasure of musical"*: Kenneway, *Bad Vibrations*, 53.

176 "The body of the sound": Hadlock, "Sonorous Bodies," 537.

178 *"The dulcet notes of the instrument"*: Zeitler, *The Glass Armonica*, 264–65.

179 *But a single individual, Bartolomeo Cristofori: The New Grove Dictionary of Music and Musicians*, "Pianoforte [piano]."

182 *Perhaps the most notable of these individuals*: Zeitler, *The Glass Armonica*, 125.

183 *"My spare Time and Attention"*: *Papers of Thomas Jefferson*, To Thomas Jefferson from Francis Hopkinson, June 28, 1786.

183 *"I am very much pleased with your project"*: *Papers of Thomas*

Jefferson, From Thomas Jefferson to Francis Hopkinson, December 23, 1786.

184 *"general mass of music compositions"*: Papers of Thomas Jefferson, xi, 141.

184 *"succeeded in making the Harmonica"*: Papers of Thomas Jefferson, To Thomas Jefferson from Francis Hopkinson, July 8, 1787.

185 *"but the tones were with difficulty produc'd"*: PBF, To the Count de Saluces, July 5, 1785.

186 *"One wants the thrill"*: Zeitler *The Glass Armonica*, 129.

9: THE ARMONICA'S REVIVAL

189 *Though the Italian composer Gaetano*: Elijah Wald, "Music of the Spheres: The Glass Harmonica," *Boston Globe Magazine*, February 25, 1996.

191 *"all the hocus-pocus"*: Ibid.

192 *"So I started saving these ends"*: Ibid.

193 *For example, the spindle in a Finkenbeiner*: Finkenbeiner and Meyer.

193 *"return from obscurity"*: Ibid.

195 All Dennis James information from my personal interview

with James, and from Ronni Reich, "Glass Armonica: Summoning the Sound of the Past," *Star-Ledger* (Newark, NJ), March 4, 2012.

203 *"I play Mozart one day and thrash rock"*: Anna Bisarra, "Thomas Bloch interview," *Time Out Hong Kong*, May 11, 2009.

ILLUSTRATION
CREDITS

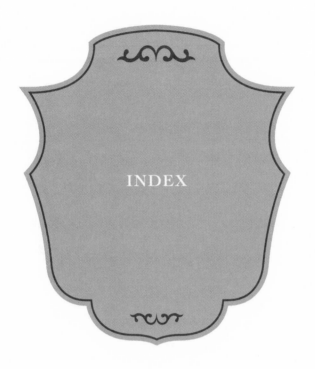

INDEX

Page numbers in *italics* refer to illustrations.

ABOUT THE AUTHOR

COREY MEAD is the author of *War Play: Video Games and the Future of Armed Conflict* and the forthcoming *The Lost Pilot: A Tale of Love and Death in the Golden Age of Aviation*. He is an associate professor of English at Baruch College, City University of New York.

Adagio

Harmon